30 Days in Heaven

Hummingbird Books

First published on the Internet (and England)

hummingbird-publishing.com

ISBN: 9798783045080

30 Days in Heaven

Mayur Kotecha

with Alison Rattle

For my parents and my Four Candles (my daughter, my son and my two nephews)

CONTENTS

PROLOGUE

My eyes flick open, and there is the sky. A washed out blue, shimmering like a bolt of silk. My face gently baking in the sun. I stare at a lone cloud drifting lazily over my head, and for the briefest of moments, I am happy.

The noises reach me first. Scooter horns, the hiss of tyres, the screech of brakes and the distant sound of sirens. Then the pain comes. I catch my breath against it. It is deep and hot and seems to be everywhere and nowhere all at once. And there is something else. Something much, much worse. I close my eyes and try to remember...

I am safe in the belly of an air-conditioned SUV. It smells sweet, of warm leather and spice. I am in the passenger seat, and I wonder if the spicy scent is the driver's aftershave. He is tapping out a beat on the steering wheel to the song he is singing in his head. He is a confident driver if a little speed-happy. So I ask him if he wouldn't mind slowing down. After all, we are in no great hurry.

"From now on, your father and I will come with you to

India for one month every year," says Mum in her 'it is decided, no arguments' voice. I turn to look at her, sitting next to Papa in the back of the car. She has closed her eyes, so she can't see the grins that spread across my face and Papa's. In that one sentence, she has put my mind at rest. Finally, there is closure between us.

But I forget that she sees everything. Even with her eyes closed. "Stop laughing at me, you two," she chides. Papa has mastered the art of staying silent during times of danger, but I am not so practised, and I can't help the boyish giggle that bubbles out of me.

I turn back around and settle into my seat. The car snakes across the road, and the driver quickly pulls it back into position. He has his phone in his hand, and it looks like he's playing some game on it. I glare at him before snatching the phone from him and setting it on the dashboard in front of me. "You can pull over at the next service station," I tell him. "Finish your game there, if you want. Then we can get on with the journey." He has the grace to apologise, at least. Mummy is snoring gently now, so I close my eyes. We will be in the car for a while yet, so I might as well get some sleep too.

I am ripped from a dream of singing and laughter by the blare of a horn crashing into my brain. I am awake in an instant. There is a beast of a vehicle overtaking us on my left. I try to gather my senses. It is all happening too quickly outside, but inside everything is slowed. I turn my head as if under water, and I see the phone in the driver's hand again. He is accelerating. But another car is pulling in front of us. I feel my mouth open in a silent scream. My body tenses as I wait for the impact. But then we are swerving the other way. A violent pull on the steering wheel and the sickening crunch of metal on metal reverberates as we hit the central reservation.

My stomach is pushed into my throat and then back again, as the car rolls over and over. My brain bangs against my skull. The image of my son floats in front of my eyes. Arjun! I cry. Arjun! And then I am spat from the car and smashed onto the tarmac.

I open my eyes, and there is the sky again. But I don't want to see the sky. I try to turn my head to one side. Slowly, slowly- it hurts so much.

I see her. I see them. I see Mummy lying on the ground close to me. She is so still. Is she still sleeping? I stare at her eyelids, willing them to flicker. I stare at her chest. Is it moving? I wait for the silk of her sari to shift as she takes a breath. But there is nothing.

I look at Papa lying next to her, and my heart clenches. He is looking back at me. Our eyes meet, and it is like he has taken me in his arms. He is smiling; his gentle, beautiful smile, and I dare to hope he is ok.

But then he is not looking at me anymore. Even though

his eyes are still open. The light has gone out. With his familiar smile still laid peacefully on his face, he drops his head, and I know that he too has gone.

ONE

"Live as if you were to die tomorrow. Learn as if you were to live forever."

- *Mahatma Gandhi*

Thirty Days Earlier.

I woke feeling marginally refreshed, which was surprising, considering how lumpy the mattress had been and how ineffective the windows were at keeping out the constant drone of traffic noise. But what did I expect from The Luxury Hotel, situated conveniently close to the airport and boasting a fine view of a concrete flyover intersection? Did a cracked window and no running hot water count as luxuries? I smiled to myself as I watched two spiders (aptly named Incy and Wincy by me the evening before) feasting on the half dozen flies they had caught so expertly in the giant web festooning one corner of the room. Nothing like fresh food at the Luxury Hotel!

It had only been a one-night stay, and I had survived it

relatively intact, which was a good result as far as I was concerned. I had a quick wash (in cold water!) and dressed in the clothes I had left out to hang the night before. I couldn't risk Mummy's eagle eyes landing on an overlooked crease. I checked my watch. There was still plenty of time to get to the airport.

I imagined Mum and Dad sitting in their plane seats (Mum would have the window seat, of course) staring out in wonder at the mountainous clouds, excited to catch a glimpse of Gujarat as the plane made its descent. They would be holding hands, naturally, and sucking furiously on a mint each. I was excited too. This trip had been a long time in planning, and I couldn't wait to show both of them the time of their lives.

I had been coming to Gujarat regularly over the years, but this was the first time my parents had joined me, and I was determined that everything should be perfect. I have a habit of being late when I am in India. It's a cultural thing, and I like to fit in. But I reasoned it would be wise to go against the custom on this occasion, so I packed my bags, handed in my keys to reception, and made my way to the airport. Sardar Vallabhbhai Patel International Airport is India's eighth busiest airport, with around 110 aircraft taking off and landing every day. It was certainly buzzing as I made my way to the terminal, checking my watch obsessively every few seconds. Airports are such strange, transient places.

They are places to be passed through - almost non-places - bursting with travellers' souls on their way to the skies. They are places of terminable boredom, too, of waiting and eating and waiting some more, where all human life and all human emotions can be witnessed alongside joyous greetings and tearful goodbyes. I was glad I was on my way to a joyous greeting.

As I approached the terminal entrance, I could see an elderly couple surrounded by luggage waiting by the doors. My heart leaped as I recognised the dear, familiar figures of my parents. Dad had that patient look of his on his face. The one he always wore when Mum was nagging him about something. After fifty-five years of marriage, I was happy to see some things never changed.

I ran towards them, and they looked up mid-argument, all words and petty grievances melting away in the warmth of the moment and the morning sun. Their eyes lit up as I held out my arms to them.

"Jai Shree Krishna Papa," I said as I wrapped my arms around Dad and hugged him close.

I turned to Mum. "Jai Shree Krishna Mummy," I said as I enveloped her in a bear hug, too. There I was, fifty-three years of age, and I was still calling her Mummy. She had never liked me using the Gujarati word for mother, "Baa," as it made her feel too old, and 'mum' was too English for her. She had always been Mummy when I addressed her directly, and she always would be.

"Jai Shree Krishna," she said with her cheek pressed to mine. Then she pushed me away to arm's length and scrutinised me with her all-seeing gaze. I half expected her to reach out and straighten my collar or to brush some imaginary dust from my shoulders. "And, why are you late?" she scolded. I saw the smile twitching at the corners of her mouth, and I wished I had hugged her first.

It was hard to believe that Dad had just turned eighty-two and Mum was seventy-four. I was in awe of their spirit and energy. They were still like a couple of teenagers, always dashing here and there, serving their religious organisation, Swadhyay Parivar, with the utmost devotion. They were tireless in their efforts to do 'God's work' and to lift the spirits of their fellow human beings. They did so much good within their community, but I often wished they would put as much care and energy into themselves and their relationship. They were no doubt devoted to each other, yet they were deeply guarded about their inner emotions. Did I ever hear Mum tell Dad she loved him? Did I ever hear him declare his love for her? I'm not sure I ever did. Yet, they were joined at the hip. They were a pair, a double act, and it was impossible to imagine one existing without the other, despite having very distinct - and very different - personalities. They were a couple always on the move, a dynamic duo, and if I could have bottled and sold just a fraction of their vitality, I would be a wealthy man indeed.

Back home in London, come rain or shine, Mum and her friend would venture out every day to walk three and a half kilometres around the park opposite our house. And if that weren't enough exercise for one day, on returning home, she would clean the house meticulously from top to bottom. Woe betides anyone who thought to help her! If you even dared to vacuum a room, she would be right there behind you cleaning it all again. Because no one, absolutely no one, could ever live up to her vigorously high standards. For the same reasons, she would never contemplate taking on any form of home help. "I would have to spend too much time training somebody," she would quip.

Mum was a fantastic and inventive cook. The best restaurants in the world could not compete with the delicious aromas curling their way languorously from out of her kitchen. She hungrily lapped up compliments, and if she was ever out in company and somebody else's dish was praised, she would scurry home to watch a few episodes of Sanjeev Kapoor's show Khanna Khazana before spending hours whipping up another totally new and delectable dish. The most celebrated face of Indian cuisine, Sanjeev Kapoor, was Mum's cookery hero, and she prided herself on her ability to emulate (and sometimes surpass) his skills in the kitchen. And of course, the lucky recipients of these mouth-watering creations were obliged to ooh and aah over every mouthful while Mummy, her face pink with pride, protested with false modesty. "It's just something I threw together."

Dad in his eighties was an altogether more chilled character than Mummy. He was an enormously humble man who didn't have her competitive temperament, being more than happy to accept whatever duties his religious organisation asked of him. He was relaxed in his old age and very encouraging of other people's achievements and ambitions. He was a far cry from the 'angry young man' of my childhood when the weight of responsibilities still lay heavy on his shoulders. I have vivid memories of my older brother and me sitting next to Dad in his car's front passenger seat, navigating the streets from a well-thumbed copy of the London A-Z. If we reached our destination without getting lost, we would receive a cherished "well done," but if we guided Dad down a wrong turning, his scolding tongue would lash us raw. There was never any need for him to punish us physically. The raising of his voice was always enough.

All these years later, I was closer to Dad than I'd ever been. He was my hero and my best friend, and I was determined to show him and Mummy the time of their lives during the precious thirty or so days we had stretching ahead of us.

TWO

"The best way to find yourself is to lose yourself in the service of others."

- *Mahatma Gandhi*

I had expected Mum and Dad to be exhausted. After all, they had just spent twenty hours travelling from London to Mumbai and then on to Ahmedabad. But, as always, I had to admire their sheer resilience, the way their eyes sparkled as they took in their surroundings, how full of child-like wonder they were, and of course, Mum's non-stop chattering. All the way to Vadodara, she talked about the wedding we were due to attend in March and how she needed to go shopping immediately for a new sari. And not any old sari either. It most definitely had to be light-blue and white, as was the current trend. As Mum said, "All the young ladies are wearing it nowadays." I smiled to myself. Even in her seventies, Mum still had her finger on the pulse. She thrived on her formidable self-belief in her youth and prided herself on keeping up with the times. Mum could outshine any fashionable twenty-year-old with her stunning outfits. And Dad, of course, after complaining about how much money she spent, indulged her in all of her whims and encouraged her to only buy the best.

With Mum amusing us with family anecdotes and gossip, we soon arrived in Vadodara, one of Gujarat's most appealing cities and its third largest. It is situated on the banks of the Vishwamitri River, which is still home to around two hundred snappy crocodiles. On the way to our hotel, I appointed myself an official tour operator and offloaded some useless facts, trying to sound as impressively knowledgeable as I could. Vadodara is also known as Baroda, I told my parents and was named after the vast number of Banyan (Vad) trees that grow there. The British changed the name to Baroda to make it easier to pronounce, but it was changed back to Vadodara in 1974. So much for attempting to sound fascinating. Mum and Dad were far more interested in catching sight of the city's elegant palaces and bustling bazaars.

After checking into our hotel, a far more up-market version than my airport hotel the night before, I prepared myself to head out on Mum's "essential sari shopping spree." But it seemed that her ambitions were greater than her physical endurance after all. Five minutes after taking her luggage into her room, she was sound asleep on the bed.

I took the opportunity to rest myself, to wash the dust from my face, to draw the curtains against the heat of the sun, and to stretch out and enjoy the feel of a lump free mattress. As I closed my eyes, I reminded myself that this trip was the first time in decades my parents would have the opportunity to truly relax. I had planned everything meticulously, down to the very last detail. I had made all their travel arrangements, booked all our accommodation, and planned our agenda. Our meals would be cooked for us, and all our laundry would be taken away and delivered back freshly washed and ironed. All Mum and Dad had to do were to come along and enjoy the ride. They had worked so hard all their lives, and they had sacrificed a life of luxury for my brother and I and our children, so it was the least I could do to try and give something back to them.

Mum and Dad were both born in East Africa - in Tanzania, to be exact. My grandparents, all from the western Indian state of Gujarat, had been lucky enough to live through the highly infectious Spanish flu pandemic that had swept through the country in 1918. The deadly flu, believed to have crept in via a ship of returning soldiers that docked in Bombay, completely ravaged India, killing between 17 and 18 million people, more than all the casualties of WW1. The virus even struck down the feted Mahatma Gandhi. Only he was lucky enough to recover. The celebrated Hindi poet and writer, Suryakant Tripathi (or Nirala) wrote about his experience of the flu pandemic, describing how he lost his wife and other family members, how they "disappeared in the blink of an eye," and of how the Ganges River was "swollen with dead bodies."

The terrible loss of life was compounded when a failed monsoon led the country into drought and famine and saw starving people pushed into the cities searching for food, which in turn stoked the spread of the killer flu. Against this backdrop, the British government opened the doors to enable semi-skilled workers from Gujarat and other regions to travel to a new life in East Africa. Their famous Gujarati entrepreneurial zeal was welcomed with open arms.

Mum and Dad were born into the thriving Gujarati community of Tanzania and first crossed paths when their prospective families arranged their marriage. It's hard to imagine them both as young people, but I remembered a story Mum once told me when I asked her if she'd liked Dad when she first met him. She smiled like a shy teenager before chuckling to herself.

"I was engaged to him," she said. "We went to his house for a meal, and towards the end of the evening, he asked your auntie to get me to meet him in another room. Remember, it was very much frowned upon to spend any time with a man before marriage, so I didn't know what to do. I was frightened and torn. Did I risk getting into trouble with the man I was due to marry in a few days, or did I risk getting into trouble with my father?" She laughed. "It was not easy being a woman in those days."

"What did you decide to do?" I asked.

"I went to meet your father, of course. Your nana looked at me in disgust as I walked to meet him, but I went to that room anyway."

I stared at her in admiration and mild shock. Imagine Mum behaving in that way! "Why did Papa call you into that room?" I asked her.

Her eyes shone as she recalled the reason. "He wanted to give me a present - a bottle of perfume. And you certainly did not give presents to each other in front of your elders! I was shaking, so I quickly grabbed the bottle and stepped back out of the door. He just had time to ask if I was happy, but I was so shy, I could only nod." She looked at me and grinned. "He was a very handsome man with such a big heart."

I grinned back at her. How amazing to imagine my parents having such a Bollywood moment. What an old romantic Dad was.

"I did get a scolding from my father later that night," Mum continued. "But I didn't care. I was going to marry a man who gave me French perfume!"

We both laughed. "Everything is sweet before marriage," I said. "And Papa has been in trouble ever since, hasn't he Mummy?"

In those days, Tanzania was still part of the British Empire, and Dad worked for a branch of the British owned Barclays Bank, which became the National Bank of Commerce when the banks were nationalised. My brother and I were born in Mwanza, as were Mum and Dad, and in 1970, when I was four years old, we moved to the town of Kigoma, the main port on the coast of Lake Tanganyika. It was also the gateway to Western Tanzania's recently established National Parks, including the Mahale Mountains, home to humanity's nearest genetic kin; wild chimpanzees. The town was pretty much cut off from the outside world as the roads were so poorly maintained, but local buses and a ferry provided transport to the countries bordering Lake Tanganyika.

We led an idyllic life. Dad's job at the bank provided us with a luxurious apartment complete with a maid and security guards. We had everything we could possibly need. Dad always used to say he never had to lift a finger. My fondest memories are of the time I spent at school there. I was a popular boy, always acting the clown but with a propensity for lateness that was often punished by the sharp rap of a ruler across my knuckles. The joker in me could not resist trying to outwit my teacher by pulling my hand away at the last minute. This daredevil act resulted in the laughter I craved from my classmates and an extra rap for my knuckles. But as I cared more about amusing my friends, the knuckle rapping was neither here nor there. Then came the day when, once again late for class, I walked directly up to my teacher, Mr Joseph, with my hand held out ready and willing to take my punishment, with the usual defiant grin on my face. But this time, he turned the tables on me. "Young man," he said with a smile. "Never again will I cane my most mischievous student. Thank God the government has now permitted you to be late for school."

That certainly stopped me in my tracks. The five-year-old Mayur was furious. How dare this teacher and the government ruin my reputation like that? How dare he take away my opportunity to be the centre of attention, to be the comedian on stage, to be firmly in the spotlight? He was a clever man, Mr Joseph.

You may think that having a brother only fifteen months older meant I had a ready-made playmate, but this was not the case. Outside of school, I preferred to spend my time with Nasreen, the girl next door, and the sister I never had. We spent all our time together, playing badminton, hide and seek and generally fooling around. The truth was, I was scared of my brother. He might have been only fifteen months older than me, but I was expected to obey him. "He is your elder brother," my parents told me. He knows what is best for you. You have to listen to him."

Unfortunately for me, my brother took his responsibilities seriously. To put it mildly, he made my life hell. He drummed it into me that I was a total waste of space, and when I was only four, he informed me that God would not be happy with me unless I licked the soles of his shoes. Who knows what dirt and unmentionables I ingested in doing his bidding. "God will punish you if you do not do as I say," he told me as my tongue lapped at his feet. "God will only be happy if you obey me."

A year or so later, after outgrowing the education on offer in Kigoma, we were both shipped off to the bustling metropolis of Dar es Salaam to continue our schooling. The city of Dar es Salaam straddles some of the most important sea routes in the world and has the second busiest port in East Africa. It was a colourful, noisy, eclectic place, and for two young boys sent away from home for the first time, it was a pretty scary experience.

Having only each other for company for the first time in our lives, my brother and I became quite close. I'd always had the knack of making friends quickly and easily, whereas my brother was a loner with very few friends, and now he had no one else except me. We lived with a family, friends of my parents, and although they were kind and made us feel welcome, they were not very well off, so there was less food on the table than we were used to (despite Dad paying them generously), and our stomachs often rumbled with hunger. At the end of each school day, and knowing there would be a long wait until dinner, I got into the habit of stealing a couple of spiced cucumbers from a guy with a food stall outside the school gates. My brother was only too happy to share my ill-gotten gains, but whenever we went back home to Kigoma, he would grass me up to our parents, earning me a tongue-lashing and a lecture on the error of my ways. We only spent ten months in Dar es Salaam in the end. But I remember those months as being among the happiest times I spent with my brother. I had him all to myself, I had his attention, and I had the brother I had always wished for.

The time came when my parents had to make the most important decision of their lives. Although my brother and I were doing fine at school, the education system in Tanzania was not all it could have been, and they wanted better for us. The one place they knew that could provide us with the level of education they desired was England. But to move to England, they would have to sacrifice almost everything.

And that is exactly what they did. When I was just eight years old, we moved to Leicester, England, as illegal immigrants. Dad had only two hundred pounds to his name, and Mum had to sell all her jewellery. My parents struggled tremendously for the first three years, with Dad working every hour under the sun, shifting heavy boxes in a supermarket. Eventually, he proved he had the means to support himself and his dependents, and we were granted the right to stay. Dad secured himself a managerial position at the Bank of Credit and Commerce in South London, and our fortunes turned considerably. He was a shrewd but enormously modest man. He didn't spend his money on flash clothes or flash cars (although Mummy would have loved him too!); instead, he focussed on securing his children's futures, gifting both my brother and me deposits to buy our houses, and later paying tens of thousands of pounds towards his four grandchildren's university costs. I began to understand why Dad was the way he was when I learned he had lost his own father when he was just a child. My grandfather passed away in 1946, leaving Dad, at the tender age of eight, as the man of the house. Dad would sometimes tell me how he, his mother, and two little sisters struggled financially and how there was often only salted boiled rice to eat. This experience turned Dad into the enormously generous human being that he was. The more successful he became and the more money he made, the more he gave away. He could live with the bare necessities as long as he provided for his family.

As I lay on the hotel bed with all these thoughts drifting through my sleepy head, I felt my heart almost burst with gratitude. Our lives had been far from perfect. As in every family, we had gone through difficult times, dark times, and there were still various tensions simmering ominously under the surface. But I couldn't have been blessed with more caring, loving parents, and for the next thirty days, I was going to concentrate all my efforts on giving them both the best time possible, even though it would be just a fraction of what they had given me.

THREE

"A nation's culture resides in the hearts and in the soul of its people."

- *Mahatma Gandhi*

After a couple of hours of sleep, Mum and Dad were raring to go again. Not wishing to push them too hard, I decided, on that first evening, to take them to the cinema. We stepped out into the balmy air, revelling in the sights, sounds, and scents of our surroundings. The most common way for Indian families to travel is by rickshaw. For those that take this form of transport every day, it is no big deal. But for those of us living in the west, the thrill of a rickshaw ride is akin to riding the dodgem cars at a fairground. We sat in the back, holding on tight, while the autowalah wove the rickshaw from left to right, narrowly avoiding colliding with other vehicles as well as wandering cows, stray dogs, and pedestrians. If the city were ever to succumb to a heart attack one day, it would definitely be down to the number of rickshaws clogging up its arteries. Our teeth rattled, our bones shook, but as this was the first time we had ever ridden together like this, I knew I had to capture the moment with a selfie. I didn't have to tell Mum and Dad to smile. They were already grinning like a couple of over-excited kids. And all this for forty rupees!

When the autowalah dropped us off outside the cinema, Mum was still grinning as I helped her down. "Pay the man," she said.

"Should Mummy and Papa pay, or the baby?" I joked.

She burst out laughing and grabbed my wallet. Papa was standing behind the rickshaw, laughing even louder. I didn't think my joke had been that funny, but then he pointed to a sign hanging on the back of the vehicle, which read, "Capacity 3 idiots." That was it. All three of us collapsed into a fit of giggles. It was a rare and beautiful moment. The three of us united in humour and mirth. We laughed even louder when we realised the autowalah had left without giving us our change.

The cinema in India is a whole different experience from the cinemas in the UK. It is not just about the movie; it is all about eating too - feasting on a film and feasting on food. There is a mind-boggling array of delicious delicacies on offer from pizza, Bombay sandwiches oozing with chutney, spices, and cheese, masala noodles, masala sweetcorn, and cheese frankies, to pani puri, dahi puri, sev puri, aloo tikka chat, bhel puri chat and of course popcorn and fizzy drinks. There is no standing in long queues either. You simply place your order along with your ticket number, and the food is delivered to the comfort of your seat.

As I watched Mum and Dad arguing over what they would like to eat, I smiled to myself, remembering the occasions they took me to the cinema as a child. I had been far less trouble and a whole lot more obedient than they were!

"I'm not hungry," said Mum. "I won't eat much. But I will have a coke though."

Did I hear correctly? Mum ordering a coke? When at home in London, this is the woman who would loudly proclaim to all her friends that she never drank fizzy drinks, as they were so unhealthy. Yet here she was, taking delicate sips through a colourful straw of the sparkling, syrupy drink. I was glad she had relaxed into holiday mode enough to let the veneer of snobbery drop.

I was famished. I hadn't eaten while Mum and Dad slept, as I hadn't known what time they would wake up, and I didn't want to eat without them. Taking on board the fact that Mum said she wasn't hungry and being the ever-dutiful son, I ordered a couple of small portions of masala noodles. One for Mummy on my left and one for Papa on my right - so at least they had something to nibble on. "Have some," Dad said, pushing his dish towards me.

"No, no. You eat. I had something when you were sleeping," I fibbed. Fifteen minutes later, a couple of cheese frankies arrived. These are a hugely popular type of street food, consisting of a soft roti wrap containing a mixture of spicy vegetables, zingy salad, drizzles of chutney, and plenty of melted cheese. The smell alone is enough to make your taste buds sing. Mummy offered me one of these delicious concoctions, and although my stomach was crying out for food, I wanted her to enjoy it more. So I shook my head. "I ate while you were sleeping," I fibbed again.

So Mummy on the left of me had one, and Papa on my right had one. While poor 6ft. 3inch baby in the middle felt like calling Childline! By the time the interval arrived, I could no longer ignore the hunger growling around in my stomach like a mad dog on the loose. I rushed downstairs to beat the crowd and ordered masala noodles, cheese frankie, bhel puri chat, and spicy sweet corn, and three cokes, just in case. I paid extra as an incentive for speedy delivery, and when the food arrived, Papa shook his head at me and smiled while Mummy gave her little boy a well-deserved lecture.

The cinema in India is immensely popular; with over 1800 movies produced every year. Bollywood, the Hindi language film industry, evolved separately from Hollywood, and the movies account for almost half of all box office revenue. They are known for their unique aesthetics, the most striking examples being song and dance, romantic melodrama, and elaborate set designs. The songs from these movies live on as pop hits, and everywhere you go, you can hear this music blaring out onto the streets from shops, restaurants, bars, and rickshaws. The excitement created by these popular films and songs is palpable and seeps into every area of life. I once had a barber shave me with a cut throat razor while he was swaying along in beat to some Bollywood tune. Needless to say, he did not receive a tip from me that day.

Our movie of choice that day was a Gujarati film called "Chaal Jivi Liye." It was a comedy and a tearjerker road-trip drama exploring the relationship between a loving father and an ambitious workaholic son. In his quest to become a successful entrepreneur, Aditya puts his personal life on the back burner, never coming home on time and never spending any time with his father, Bipin. Despite Bipin pleading with Aditya to change his ways for the sake of his health and so that father and son can spend some time together, Aditya ignores him. He continues to push himself to the limit in his desire for global success. He eventually collapses from stress and is sent to a top hospital to be seen by an eminent doctor, a friend of Bipin's. After examining Aditya closely, the doctor tells him there is nothing wrong that a good rest won't cure.

The doctor then turns to Bipin. Apparently, he has avoided all his routine health check-up appointments, so the doctor insists that he might as well examine him there and then. It turns out that Bipin has a tumour, known as pontine glioma, and only a month left to live, at the most. Of course, Aditya is floored by this news. When Bipin asks him to spend the remaining time accompanying him on a trip to the Himalayas, where he honeymooned with Aditya's mother and where Aditya was conceived, there is no way his son can refuse. On the way, they meet a girl called Ketki, and the three of them set out on the most unexpected and most satisfying journey of their lives.

Partway through the movie, the actors sang the song, Pa pa pagli. The beautiful, heart-rending lyrics included words that many Gujarati fathers sing to their babies as they take their first steps holding on to Papa's fingers. Dad and I exchanged knowing looks, each of us transported back in time. I wondered if Dad remembered singing those words to my brother and me? I certainly remembered us singing them to my own children. My heart ached. The pain of missing my children was sharp and raw.

The movie continued with the unfolding of a beautiful bonding between the son and his father, but with an incredible twist that had the whole cinema reaching for the tissues. It turned out that it was Aditya who was terminally ill and not his father. Using his influence over his friend, Bipin had persuaded the doctor not to reveal the truth to Aditya. By pretending to be ill himself and under the pretext of fulfilling his last dreams and wishes, Bipin was able to dupe his son into putting aside his business interests and living a life with true meaning for the short time he had left. And, of course, he got to spend that special time bonding with his son.

We were all mopping our eyes by the end. But little did I know that only thirty-one days later, it would only be me, the son, left alive. That movie and that song became embedded in my heart when I finally regained consciousness in hospital a couple of months later.

FOUR

"Work is undoubtedly worship, but laughter is life. Anyone who takes life too seriously must prepare himself for a miserable existence. Anyone who greets joy and sorrows with equal facility can really get the best of life."

- *Sardar Vallabhbhai Javerbhai Patel*

We were more than happy to have a couple of days to spare in Vadodara. I was hoping it would give Mum and Dad a chance to really get into the spirit of relaxation. Chilling out was such an alien concept to those two. I persuaded them to spend another evening feasting at the cinema and to avoid any arguments, I went ahead and organised a trip out for the following day.

"A taxi will be here to pick us up at nine in the morning," I informed them. "It's about a two-hour drive to get to the statue of Sardar Valabhbhai Patel."

Dad's eyes widened with interest. "The new statue? Is it finished already?" He was as excited as a young schoolboy and went directly to the hotel reception to book an alarm call for 8 o'clock the following morning. "No Indian timing," he told the bemused receptionist. "8 o'clock is 8 o'clock. No, you listen to me. I was a bank manager, and I did not open the bank late once. 8 o'clock is 8 o'clock. What time are you going to wake me? Good. Thank you, beta."

Mum was less enthusiastic. She stuck her bottom lip out. "I don't want to go to some silly old statue," she said. "Why do you want to drive for two hours just to see a statue?"

"If you don't want to come, we can drop you off at Santaben's house in the morning," Dad said, slipping me a quick wink.

"Yes, Mummy," I said. "It's okay. You can stay here at Santaben's." Santaben was one of Mum and Dad's closest friends, and I knew Mum would have just as lovely a time staying behind, but I had a trick up my sleeve to persuade her to join us. "I hear your friend from your religious group has visited the statue," I said slyly. "She said it was such a fabulous experience, and she really enjoyed herself. It's the tallest statue in the world, you know."

Mum's ears pricked up, and her nose twitched. "What? She never told me she had been. When did she go? Well, if you are insisting, okay, we will go. It's not fair for the driver to cancel now. When did she go, did you say?"

I knew I would be in big trouble with that particular friend. But at least Mum could tell her how very wonderful her visit to the statue had been.

Sardar Vallabhbhai Patel is known as the "Ironman" of India. He played a vital role in India's struggle for independence and the later integration of over 500 princely states into the Union of India. Sardar in Gujarati and most Indian languages means leader or chief. The women of Bardoli bestowed this title on Patel after he led them in the 1928 Bardoli Satyagraha, a movement in the independence struggle by the farmers of Bardoli against the unjust raising of taxes.

After years of suffering from floods and famines, the farmers of Bardoli were left facing financial ruin. They appealed to the Governor of Bombay Presidency to have their taxes reduced. The government refused this request and saw fit to raise the farmer's taxes by a further 30%.

Left on the brink of starvation, the farmers turned to Patel to help lead them in a revolt. Patel warned them that by refusing to pay their taxes, they could be thrown in jail and have their lands and properties confiscated. But the farmers were resolute. They were ready to unite to take a non-violent stand against government injustices by withholding their taxes. The British Raj was furious and vowed to crush the revolution. They stormed the villages, seized land and properties, and put them up for auction. But not one single person from across India came forward to buy the confiscated lands. And in another glorious twist, when Indian members of the Government in Bombay and across

India began to resign from office in support of the farmers, the Raj had no choice but to back down and agree to the farmer's terms.

All land and property were restored, and all taxes were waived for a year. Patel modestly credited the farmers' grit and determination and the teachings of Mahatma Gandhi for the victory. But people from across India recognised his vital role as leader and bestowed him with the title Sardar.

Patel became a member of the Indian national Congress alongside Mahatma Gandhi, Jawaharlal Nehru, and Mohammed Ali Jinnah, the founder of the state of Pakistan. Together they fought for the independence of India from Britain. Once independence was established, Jinnah fought the other three for Pakistan's independence, and once that was assured, there was yet more in fighting over who should be voted first Prime Minister of free India. Sardar Vallabhbhai Patel was the most popular choice, but for various political reasons, the role went to Jawaharlal Nehru. According to Nehru's biographer, Michael Brecher, "In accordance with the time-honoured practice of rotating the Presidency, Patel was in line for the post. Fifteen years had elapsed since he presided over the Karachi session, whereas Nehru had presided at Lucknow and Ferozpur in 1936 and 1937. Moreover, Patel was the overwhelming choice of the Provincial Congress Committees.... Nehru's "election" was due to Gandhi's intervention. Patel was persuaded to step down....If Gandhi had not intervened, Patel would have been the first de facto Premier of India, in 1946-7....Sardar was "robbed of the prize," and it rankled deeply."

I knew Dad felt the same. As the taxi drove us towards Kevadiya, where the statue of Patel (The Statue of Unity) is situated, he was in a particularly impassioned mood. "Every member of Congress voted for Patel to be the first Prime Minister," he stated. "But Nehru was adamant. He would not relent at a time of grave crisis for India. But Patel was the bigger man. For the sake of our country, which was in danger of losing more land, he stepped aside. But we had the wrong leader in Nehru. And it cost the country dearly."

Dad had got into his stride. His eyes danced as he expounded on one of his favourite topics, while Mum chose to feign boredom and amused herself by making the odd aside to the driver about the passing scenery.

"Nehru cost the country dearly," continued Dad. "Corruption took over on a national scale from the very top down to grassroots level. Patel dedicated his life to the cause of India. But Nehru sold India out. If we can travel freely today across the beautiful and bountiful lands of India, it is because of Sardar Vallabhbhai Patel."

I could see why Dad was so excited by our outing. Patel was his childhood hero, and Dad was elated that the present Prime Minister had seen fit to elevate him from the insignificant annals of British and Indian history, and to establish him as the true champion of Indian Independence by erecting a 182 metre high statue (almost twice the height of the Statue of liberty and 29 metres taller than the second tallest Spring Temple Buddha statue in China) in his honour.

During all my own political ruminations, I have concluded that what we really need is a party of Martians to beam down to Earth to help us sort out our differences. If you think about it for a moment, England was once made up of small independent countries all fighting against each other. Then they united to fight against the Scottish. As soon as France and the Spanish Armada threatened the British coastline, the whole of the British Isles united to engage in a two-hundred-year sea battle with these two powers. Britain and France then united to fight the Germans. Twice. The French, British, and half of the Germans along with the Americans, then all united to oppose the Soviet Union. And meanwhile, the arms manufacturers raked in the profits for over a couple of thousand years. It was no different in India. All the princely states fought each other for greed, glory, and power. Even after the great battle of Kurukshetra - the battle to end all battles - with regions of Aryan and Dravidian states witnessing the slaughter of entire armies, the fighting did not stop. Centuries down the line, Hindu India was invaded and overwhelmed by the Moghuls bringing with them the religion of Islam. Centuries of Hindu-Muslim fighting came to a pause. Then the British arrived and overstayed their welcome by a couple of centuries. "There must be Hindu-Muslim unity always. We must drive the British out together," is a famous quote from the movie Gandhi.

So then what happens? The British are finally driven out after two hundred years of robbing India, and the Hindus and Muslims start fighting each other. The Muslims that wanted their own country got their own country. This left the Indian Congress leaders fighting with each other as to who should lead the country. Yep, we definitely need aggressive Martians (as in the movie Independence Day) to land on Earth, so the human race can finally unite, regardless of colour, race, religion, border, or gender.

Maybe the truth is that Martians did come in peace but took one look at the crazy human race and fled to Venus, where they found their true soul mates!

I saw Dad's eyes dampen with emotion as he caught sight of the Statue of Unity from inside the taxi. If nothing else, the sheer size of it was cause for admiration. Even the location of the statue is a cause for wonder. It stands majestically on Sadhu Island, a short distance from the celebrated Valley of Flowers; a 17km trail of colourful, jewel-like flowers blooming along the banks of the holy River Narmada. The flowers are planted in such as way as to resemble a rainbow on Earth: Red, yellow, white, pink, and gold. There are over a hundred varieties of flowers from Gulmohar, Pongaro, Bonganveliya, and Nerium to masses of multi-hued grasses, marigolds, vinca, and sunflowers. If Mum wasn't impressed by a mere 182 metre high statue, she couldn't help having her breath taken away by the sight of this wondrous carpet of flowers.

Dad continued to lecture us as we stood on the travellator, taking us towards the statue. "It is a great symbol of India's engineering and technical capabilities," he pronounced. "It cost nearly £40 million and took five years to build." He squinted into his guidebook. "The height of the statue was fixed at 182 metres to denote the total democratic assembly constituencies in the state of Gujarat. Oh, and listen," he said excitedly. "The base of the statue is made from over 129 tonnes of scrap iron, donated by nearly 100 million farmers from across India, and the whole construction can withstand wind velocity up to 60 metres per second and earthquakes measuring below 6.5 on the Richter scale."

Mum and I rolled our eyes at each other. She looked out at the stunning scenery and sighed. "You really love India, don't you?"

"Yes, Mummy," I said. "I feel as if my heart is truly happy when I am here." I was so lucky to spend six months of the year in this wonderful country and the remaining six months living with Mum and Dad in London. Although they were extremely independent and self-sufficient, there was no denying they were getting on now, and they needed that extra bit of support and the comfort of knowing there was somebody else there to look out for them. The six-monthly arrangement was perfect. It was enough to give them a certain level of confidence, but they also had some freedom from their baby son, whose constant presence might have seriously cramped their style.

Living with my parents brought mixed blessings. On the one hand, we shared many happy times together, but on the other hand, there were some tough challenges to face. I had many anger issues to deal with, regarding Mum's meddling in my marriage, her silence over my brother's ill treatment of Dad, and her complete denial of any wrongdoing. Also, living with them shone a light on their relationship, and I came to see its mechanics. I saw how Mum was never disloyal to Dad but never attempted to be his friend either. I saw how their marriage was a love-hate relationship, with neither of them ever at peace with each other. The fighting and arguing between them was almost continuous, yet they would never have contemplated leaving each other. It was strange, though. Now they were here with me in India, with no other outside influences, where they could have fought day and night with no one to phone up and complain about the other to; there had not been one single bust up. I could only put it down to the jet lag!

We followed Dad into the museum at the base of the statue. It was equipped with state-of-the-art audio-visual systems for visitors to gain an inspiring insight into the life of Sardar Valabhai Patel. Mum and I hovered behind Dad as he listened to each and every recorded speech of his hero. As I stood watching him absorb all these historical stories, I realised for the first time that I must have inherited my love of history from him.

There were only so many political speeches that Mum could pretend to be interested in, and eventually, we left Dad to his own devices, and I took Mum to sit and rest on a nearby bench. I was all ready to hear her complain about Dad's obsession with Indian independence, but to my surprise, she didn't utter a single word against him. I laughed to myself. Jet lag must really hit the elderly hard!

For the next hour, we sat and chatted. It had been a long while since it had just been the two of us, and it reminded me how it had been when I was a child. Mum focussed her attention on me - my romance with India and my life in general. "Why don't you get married here?" she asked. "It would be perfect."

I smiled. "I've already been down that route twice, Mummy." It was true. I had one official wedding and the other, a Hindu fire ceremony at the foot of the Himalayas. "I'm much better at just having a girlfriend, Mummy. It's much easier to untangle yourself from than a marriage."

At that point in my life, I was still recovering from the after effects of two failed marriages, and I genuinely believed that having a "girlfriend" was far less complicated.

Having a girlfriend meant being able to enjoy the thrill of dating, dining out, going to movies and the theatre, and generally making an effort. But it also gave you the freedom to meet the lads at the cricket club on a Friday night, to go to the gym, to football matches, and to hear those magical words. "I like you just the way you are. I never want you to change." Words, which to my mind, always seemed to fade away after the marriage vows were taken, like mist evaporating in the heat of the morning sun.

Mum was not one to give up easily. "Your second wife was nice," she said. "She still likes you. And she likes India too."

"I know, Mummy," I said. "And we are still the best of friends. We love each other, and I will always cherish the six years I had with her. Those years will always have a special place in my heart. But we were too different for the marriage to have worked."

"There is nothing wrong with being different," she countered. "No two people are the same. Look at your Papa and me."

Indeed, I thought. A powerful statement with no answer required. "I'm not like Papa," I said. "I don't have his tolerance."

She prickled at this. "Huh. You always see faults in me, don't you? As if your father is perfect." She set her mouth in a tight line.

"Mummy, we are on holiday," I said, trying to halt the conversation. "Let's just enjoy ourselves."

After a while, of talking about this and that and nothing in particular, Mum poked me in my side. "Hey, what about that girl who came to visit Papa and me at home two weeks ago - Suji? The one who brought a birthday cake for Papa?"

"Ah, Mummy! Stop trying to marry me off," I laughed. "I've only known that poor girl for a short time. And, yes, I do like her. But isn't that the case at the beginning of every relationship?"

We could hear Dad's voice drifting out to us from inside the huge cinema enclosure. We strolled over and found him seated on the front bench with a gaggle of around twenty school children sat at his feet. With his soft, patient voice, he had ensnared the children's attention, and even the two teachers sitting nearby were captivated by what he had to say.

I stood to one side to watch and listen, filled with enormous pride for this man and his extensive knowledge of Indian Independence. The thought struck me that I had never made an effort to truly get to know my parents and uncover all their wonderful qualities. Dad was comparing Patel to Arjun of Mahabharat in his talk. "Nobody in the Congress dared to oppose Mahatma Gandhi when they wanted to disagree, except Valabhbhai. He spoke with earnest and for the cause of Independence. The British feared him more than

Nehru and encouraged Nehru to defy Congress for the leadership. The British also chucked in Lady Mountbatten for good measures."

The school children were bewildered. But the teachers giggled. "If it was not for Valabhbhai," Dad continued. "India would have lost more land. As the Home Minister, he dared to defy the Prime Minister. He mobilised the troops in Kashmir and Hyderabad, and he ensured the district of Junagadh was not lost. Indian history needs to be changed to recognise his greatness and Nehru's betrayal of this country."

After the children had wandered off to explore other things, one of the teachers stayed behind, chatting with Dad for a further fifteen minutes. She turned to me afterward. "Wow," she said. "I've learned more from him than from any of the other lectures. What a knowledgeable man he is."

"He certainly is," I replied, my heart swelling with love and respect for my progenitor.

Construction of the Statue of Unity finished in 2018, and it was first opened to the public in November the same year, along with the newly planted Valley of Flowers. As it was such a new tourist attraction, there were no guesthouses or hotels on-site. Still, there was an excellent indoor food court serving all manner of Gujarati delicacies alongside a considerable array of international food and a pizza stall, which, of course, we couldn't bring ourselves to bypass. We loaded up with mouth-watering dhokra, dhokra khaman, samosas, kachoris, red and green chilli sauce, and three bottles of fizzy Mountain Dew. It would be the third day in a row that Mum feasted on junk food. But what did it matter? We were on holiday, and eating out in Gujarat was a joyful experience for us. There was no cooking to be done, no washing up, and most importantly, no worries over cross-contamination as vegetarian offerings far outnumbered non-vegetarian options.

I was born into a vegetarian family. Aside from my brother and I eating meat at school for a short time after moving from Tanzania to England, we have continued to be vegetarians. A couple of years after they got married, Dad introduced Mum to the wonder of eggs, which totally enraged my grandmother. Sunday morning breakfasts were a delight for our egg-loving family. Mum soon became a master egg chef, flipping fried eggs with ease, scrambling them into creamy, golden heaps, whipping up plain omelettes and spicy omelettes, and not forgetting boiling them to simple perfection. But after listening to a religious sermon in 1981, Mum decided there were to be no more eggs in the house, and she became a hard-core vegetarian. Eating out in the UK was always a challenge. If it was not a pure vegetarian restaurant, we could not go there as a family. It was only when Mum and Dad moved from south London to north London that they discovered a wider variety of suitable restaurants. But in India, vegetarian offerings were plentiful, and we embraced the situation with unadulterated gusto.

After eating, we headed to the Valley of the Flowers, but it was all a bit too much for Papa. He had already had a most fulfilling day, so after a short stroll and a few posed photographs, he was happy to rest in a vacant security guard's chair while Mum and I continued to walk and chat and take selfies, and most importantly, tried not to fight!

Later that evening, we arrived at the cinema again. Pointing to a nearby Mumbai street food cafe, I said, "How about we eat there today? They do lovely gol gappa." Dad was easy-going, and game for anything, but Mummy had different ideas.

"What's gol gappa?" she asked.

"Pani puri."

She sniffed. "You know I don't eat junk food. Let's have masala noodles and cheese frankie. Your papa likes them too."

"Yes, Mummy." Who was I to argue?

The movie that night was "Uri – The Surgical Strike," a military action film based on actual events revolving around the surgical strike conducted by the Indian army on suspected Pakistani militants in retaliation to the 2016 Uri attack on an Indian army brigade headquarters in Jammu and Kashmir. It was perhaps not entirely up Mum's street, but Dad was enthralled, and it seemed a fitting way to end a day that had focussed on national pride. The film was a brilliant tribute to the Indian army and was packed with goose bump moments, tearful scenes, and laugh-out-loud lines. All of us, even Mum, left the cinema feeling immensely proud of our national heroes and their capabilities.

It was difficult for me to fall asleep that night. So many thoughts and emotions were churning around inside my head. I was relishing this precious time with Mum and Dad, but it was also forcing me to confront the truth of my past, the truth of my own nature, and the truth about how much my brother and Mum's behaviour had affected my life.

FIVE

"It is far better to perform one's natural prescribed duty (swadharma), though tinged with faults than to perform another's prescribed duty (paradharma), though perfectly. In fact, it is preferable to die in the discharge of one's duty than to follow the path of another, which is fraught with danger."

- *Chapter 3, Verse 35 – Bhagwad Gita*

It is a sad fact that if you are told something enough times, if it is hammered into your brain over and over again, then the illusory truth effect kicks in, and you begin to believe what you are told. You believe it to the extent that even if you are told a lie, you believe it to be the truth.

This is exactly how I came to grow up believing that I was useless. I was the useless younger brother. The dummy brother. The one who would not amount to much. The joker.

Big brother, on the other hand, was the golden boy, the blue-eyed boy, the one with all the brains. He was the one who shone in front of all our relatives, the one who was going to do so well for himself, and the one I was unfavourably compared to all the time. And as he was my big brother, and as Indian culture dictated, I had to defer to and obey him in all things.

He undoubtedly had more than me in the brain department. But then, I had much more than him in the friends' department. He was a clever boy who excelled at most subjects. And whereas I was far from stupid, I struggled in some subjects at school, except for history, at which I was a natural. I loved my history lessons and consistently achieved grade A's without even trying. While the rest of the class frantically took down notes, I would sit back with my arms folded, just listening to and absorbing the lesson. The other kids would often complain. "Sir? Why doesn't Mayur have to take notes?"

The teacher's reply – "When you start getting grades as good as Mayur's, then you can stop taking notes, too."

History was an obvious choice when choosing my A-level subjects, along with economics and law, the two other subjects I was interested in and good at. Studying history was in my swadharma – life according to my own nature. But it seemed that even in this, one of the most important decisions of my life, I had to defer to my brother. Instead of asking me what I would like to study, Dad asked my brother what he thought I should study. And straight away, he came back with the three subjects *he* excelled at; maths, chemistry, and physics - three subjects in my paradharma - outside my own nature. The best way to describe the meaning behind these two powerful Sanskrit words quoted in the Bhagwad Gita is in the following sentence: "An animal loving vegetarian can never be happy being financially successful as a butcher." The chances are you will only find happiness and success within your swadharma.

I'd always struggled with chemistry. I used to copy my friend Alpesh's homework to the extent that he got in trouble for supposedly copying mine. It was the very last subject I wanted to study at A-level, but as always, big brother was the boss. And if big brother said I had to take maths, chemistry, and physics, then I had no choice but to comply.

However, this time, I was not going to give in without a fight; a sneaky, behind-the-scenes fight. I knew it wouldn't go down well with Dad if I told him I wanted to study history to become a history teacher. In our culture, you couldn't say you wanted to be a history teacher. Most parents pushed their children towards careers in accountancy, engineering, and medicine. Promising, solid, respectable, and most of all, boast-to-the-neighbours careers. But a history teacher? No. That just didn't cut the mustard.

When the school handed out the forms for our A-level choices, which our parents had to fill in and sign, I decided to practice a little forgery. I filled in the form with my chosen subjects - history, economics, and law - my pen hovering over the section that needed signing by a parent. I had practiced Dad's signature a few times on scraps of paper that I ripped up and binned, and I was sure my attempts were passable. So, I took a deep breath and committed pen to paper. The signature was perfect, and I felt confident I had just successfully ensured the future of my education and career.

How wrong could I be? Soon enough, my brother found out what I had done and grassed me up (as they say) to Dad. My dreams of studying history were confined to, well, history, and all I had to look forward to were years of battling with subjects that were totally against my nature. It was no surprise that I failed the course three times before finally passing on the fourth attempt.

SIX

Krishna says, "Look at Me, Arjuna! If I stop from work for one moment, the whole universe will die. I have nothing to gain from work; I am the one Lord, but why do I work? Because I love the world." God is unattached because He loves; that real love makes us unattached. Wherever there is attachment, the clinging to the things of the world, you must know that it is all physical attraction between sets of particles of matter — something that attracts two bodies nearer and nearer all the time and, if they cannot get near enough, produces pain; but where there is real love, it does not rest on physical attachment at all. Such lovers may be a thousand miles away from one another, but their love will be all the same; it does not die, and will never produce any painful reaction.

To attain this unattachment is almost a life-work, but as soon as we have reached this point, we have attained the goal of love and become free; the bondage of nature falls from us, and we see nature as she is; she forges no more chains for us; we stand entirely free and take not the results of work into consideration; who then cares for what the results may be?

Do you ask anything from your children in return for what you have given them? It is your duty to work for them, and there the matter ends. In whatever you do for a particular person, a city, or a state, assume the same attitude towards it as you have towards your children — expect nothing in return. If you can invariably take the position of a giver, in which everything given by you is a free offering to the world, without any thought of return, then will your work bring you no attachment. Attachment comes only where we expect a return.

- Swami Vivekananda

Although I have tried many times, I realise that I cannot love without attachment. It is impossible for me. But I always remember the first time I truly fell in love as though it was only yesterday.

I was twenty-two, and still at university. The Easter holidays had come around, and I was feeling somewhat emotionally battered. Due to some unfortunate misunderstanding, a new relationship with a girl I thought I really liked led to a sudden break-up. She was someone I had met at university. Someone who I thought liked me as much as I liked her. But it was not to be, and my young heart was aching and filled with the misery of believing I had lost someone special.

To take my mind off her, and so that I wouldn't stay locked in my room nursing a broken heart all holiday, I decided at the last minute to go on a short trip to North Wales organised by my parents' religious group. The date was 1st April 1988, April Fool's Day. I have revisited that day in my mind over and over again throughout the years, and I still can't decide whether it was my lucky day or my unlucky day, as it was the day I met the woman who was to become my wife, the mother of my children, and then my ex-wife.

A small group of us booked onto the trip, and as we piled onto the minibus, I took little notice of my travelling companions as I was still too wrapped up in my woes and feeling sorry for myself. I stared out of the window at the passing scenery, daydreaming about what could have been, what I could have done differently, and wondering if I was ever going to meet the girl I would spend the rest of my life with. It was warm on the bus, the air filled with companionable chatter, and as we sped along the roads, I felt myself relax into the soothing motion of travel. It was then that I first set eyes on her.

She was sitting a few seats down from me. I could see her reflection clearly in the bus window, where a black canopy hung down from the roof outside. Although it must have obscured her view of the outside world, this black canopy provided me an unwavering and sharply focussed image of her face. She was framed to perfection, and for some reason, I couldn't tear my gaze away.

She was stunning, with a mesmerizing smile that not only lit up her whole face but seemed to light up the whole bus, too. For the rest of the trip, the scenery outside was forgotten, as to me, this girl was far more beautiful than anything I would see out of the window.

Once we arrived at our destination and clambered off the bus, I noticed her struggling to lift her suitcase. Although we were only staying in Wales for the weekend, it looked as though she had packed enough for a three-month stay. I stepped in immediately and offered my assistance. It was the perfect opportunity to be a gentleman. She had come with a group of friends, and they all spoke to me in Gujarati, thanking me for my help and asking if I actually understood the language. As it was April Fool's day, I couldn't resist playing around a little and joked that I was Punjabi. The joke fell flat when she revealed that she already recognised me, as her father's sister was married to my Dad's cousin. Who was the April Fool at that moment, I wonder? Needless to say, my heart had already miraculously healed and was now beating fast for a girl whose name I didn't even know yet.

The following day we all rendezvoused in the vicinity of Mount Snowdon, kitted out in our walking gear in anticipation of an exhilarating day. It was cold, but the sky was a perfect spring blue, and the sun picked out the gold in the rocks and the surrounding hills and grasses. The views were serene yet breathtaking, but in my eyes did not compare to this girl's beauty. Her name was Sia, and she was nineteen years old. She wore her hair loose that day, and it cascaded over her shoulders in shimmering waves and blew into her eyes as we tramped up a hill. She was transfixed by the scenery as much as I was transfixed by her. As we hiked up a hill, she lost her footing for a moment and fell into a stream. She wasn't hurt, but she soon began to shiver as the cold wind chilled her wet clothes. Nobody rushed to her rescue. Nobody offered her a coat or a warm jumper, or an item of dry clothing. Nobody, except me, of course.

Like a hero from a Bollywood movie, stepping forward to rescue the heroine, I offered her my leather jacket, which she accepted gratefully. With my usual brand of humour, I asked her to be careful not to fall again as the leather jacket was a gift from my brother and was one of my most valuable possessions. He had bought it for me with money from his first wage packet: a beautiful gesture that meant the world to me. My Bollywood moment didn't last for long. I was soon shivering, too, but when Sia turned her smile on me and thanked me for the jacket, I immediately forgot my cold discomfort. I was happy to face any amount of Arctic-like weather or to even catch pneumonia just for the warmth of one of her smiles.

On the way back to base, Sia took the initiative to sit next to me. It was one of those rare, wonderful moments that made me feel like a prince among men. Everything else in my world seemed to fade away, leaving just her, sitting next to me shining as brightly as the sun.

I must have made a good impression as Sia's sister approached me the next day and casually suggested that I go and talk to her. The weather that day was gloriously warm, and we were all hanging out enjoying ice creams. I must have looked like some sort of idiot, with my vanilla cone melting and dripping down my hand as I stood with my mouth open, unable to believe what I was hearing. My heart thumped loudly against my ribs as I asked Sia's sister, "Does she like me?"

She smiled and nodded, and I glanced over to Sia, hardly able to believe it could be true. She was perfect. I could never have dreamt up anyone as perfect. And she actually liked me, too!

In my mind, I was transported back into another Bollywood movie. Romantic music played loudly, and all the dancers were twirling around me, the silk of their costumes swishing through the air and their jewellery jangling in rhythm. I was in seventh heaven, but I tried my best to play it cool.

We were about to set off on another hill walk, so I grabbed the opportunity for some private time with her. "I hear you like me?" I muttered pathetically.

She giggled. "Is that the best chat up line you can come up with?"

Her voice was the sweetest I had ever heard. The calmness of it reached into my very soul and overpowered my senses. As unbelievable as it sounds, I had fallen for this girl hard in such a small space of time. I couldn't tear my eyes away from her. I wasn't experienced or practised in "chatting up" girls, I certainly wasn't a smooth operator, but somehow my clumsy efforts brought me the answer I was looking for. After walking for a while, we separated ourselves from the rest of the group and found a secluded spot where we sat down to continue getting to know each other. It wasn't long before the chatting turned into kissing. We lost sight of all time and place. We could have been anywhere in the world; it wouldn't have mattered. We were so engrossed in each other; I wished we could have stayed there forever, in our own little bubble. And maybe, we would have stayed there for longer, except we both suddenly had the strangest feeling someone was watching us. We turned around to discover our instincts were correct. We did indeed have an audience. A herd of sheep had gathered around us and were staring intently, in their sheep-like manner, as if to say, "Hey, Dude. What's happening here, man?"

It was a bizarre but memorable moment and led us in later years to find much humour in the saying, "I love ewe."

On the way back down the hill, I was acutely aware of

how strong my feelings were for Sia. As an old-fashioned kind of guy, and knowing that I wanted an "until death do us part" relationship, I made these feelings clear. But had I said too much? Had I scared her off?

"I'm not an expert in the art of conversing with a woman," I told her. "Especially not one as beautiful as you. I'm very inexperienced in these matters, and I didn't realise that you don't talk about marriage on a first date."

Luckily, she felt the same way about me. That, or she just wanted to get her hands on my costly leather jacket. Either way, that day marked the beginning of a fourteen-year-long relationship. How could she have known that I was not the most confident person in the world, having had a challenging childhood and denied the freedom to choose my own path in life? And how could I have known that her childhood challenges and traumas would make all my troubles pale into insignificance and that her self-confidence was at an even lower ebb than mine? Those discoveries were yet to come.

Our first official date took place in a five star Italian restaurant in Milton Keynes not long after returning from North Wales. Her sister accompanied her as a chaperone, but we managed to drop her back home after an hour. It was bliss to be alone together. I discovered Sia had never tried pasta, and although she had tasted pizza in the past, this was her first experience at an Italian restaurant. It was wonderful to see how much she enjoyed her meal. Afterward, we strolled around the banks of Willen Lake doing all the things that loved-up couples do; throwing bread to the swans, laughing, joking, and holding hands. We sat for a while in the Peace Pagoda, absorbing its spiritual message. There are similar pagodas all across Asia, often built in places that need the most healing, such as Hiroshima and Nagasaki. They are Buddhist monuments built as symbols of world peace and are meant to promote unity among people across the world regardless of border, race, or creed. This one in Milton Keynes was the first to be built in the western world. It was built by the monks and nuns of the Nipponzan Myohoji spiritual movement, and enshrined sacred relics of Lord Buddha from Nepal, Sri Lanka, and Berlin. Its decorative frieze told Buddha's story from his birth at the foot of the Himalayas 2,500 years ago to his death in Kusinagara after fifty years of teaching.

Surrounding the pagoda were cherry trees planted to commemorate victims of war, and nearby the One World Tree hung with prayers, small ornaments, and messages of hope for loved ones lost.

We spent a magical hour in this special place, enjoying each other's company so much that we didn't realise the evening had fallen so quickly. We were hungry again, so we wandered over to the restaurant by the lake, where Sia, much to my amusement, ordered another pasta dish while I had a veggie burger and chips. We chatted away as she proceeded to pinch most of my chips, and afterward, I ordered a fried ice cream covered in batter and toffee sauce. As I tried to figure out the 'fried ice cream' concept, Sia helped herself to almost half of my dessert too! It was time to take her home, but we managed another hour and a half of 'romancing' in the car before she reluctantly said goodbye and waved me off from her front doorstep. At which point, I drove straight back to the restaurant and ordered myself another fried ice cream.

We kept in touch every day after that, and a month later, Sia (after telling her parents she was going to a work training event) came to visit me at my university in Wales. The day before her arrival, I was like a mad man, cleaning my room from top to bottom. It looked like a typical student room, more like a store cupboard than a bedroom, with clothes and papers and dirty dishes strewn everywhere. I gathered everything up from the floor and stored it out of sight in a friend's room, then went shopping for posh snacks and fancy bottles of every non-alcoholic beverage I could find. My hard work paid off. Sia was most impressed with my accommodation and even better, she formed the opinion that I was extremely tidy and organised. I was more than happy to let her go along with that idea, at least for the time being.

We made the most of our time alone in that room. We became truly intimate for the first time, and although it was then I understood Sia was not a virgin, it didn't unduly bother me as I had never had that orthodox way of thinking. All that mattered to me was the beauty of the moment, the union of our minds and bodies, the two becoming one.

I took Sia to the beach at Porthcawl the next day. We kicked off our shoes and walked across the long, sweeping sands, dipping our toes into the sea and squealing at the cold shock. I photographed her posing on a rock, looking divine in her jeans and a white jacket. Later I would have my favourite photograph of her blown up and made into an A2 size poster. That evening we snuggled up next to each other in the local cinema to watch "Who Framed Roger Rabbit" and eat a bucket of popcorn. We were a couple of giggling teenagers holding hands in the dark.

The following day we drove to the sprawling and historically fascinating town of Merthyr Tydfil, ringed and pocked with quarries and spoil heaps from its days as the world's largest ironworks. From there, we paid a visit to Castell Coch, a medieval castle rising from an ancient forest like a vision from a fairy-tale. It was here we carried on what we had left off the month before, surrounded by sheep on a beautiful hillside. For the first and only time in my life, I knew what true love was.

When it was time for Sia to return home, I couldn't bear to just drop her off at the train station. I was a man intoxicated by the sweet poison of love, so instead, I drove a six-hour round trip to take her back to Milton Keynes.

We continued our love affair by phone and post. I would regularly receive letters from Sia drenched in her favourite perfume (and now my favourite perfume) – Paris. Just holding the envelope to my nose transported me back into her arms. She would send me small gifts of chocolates and fripperies and a tiny sheep with the words "I love ewe" stamped on its base. I treasured that silly toy so much that when my classmate accidentally broke it, he incurred my wrath for the rest of that academic year. Luckily for him, he was blessed with a superior brain that I needed to help me complete my software engineering assignments; otherwise, I doubt he would be alive today. I was a man very much in love. I had met the woman I wanted to marry and spend the rest of my life with. Little did I know back then that along with great love often comes great heartbreak.

SEVEN

"Even if you are a minority of one, the truth is the truth."

- *Mahatma Gandhi*

The great, ancient Indian epic, The Mahabharata, tells the tale of Drona, one of the greatest warriors of all time. He is rampaging through the ranks of the Pandava's, and although he is a teacher in the art of warfare to both sides and fondly revered by the Pandavas, he chooses to align himself with the Kauravas. The Pandavas fear that if Drona isn't stopped, their army will soon be destroyed. Yudhisthira, the eldest of the five Pandava brothers, turns to their spiritual and philosophical mentor Krishna for counsel.

Krishna, the eighth avatar of Vishnu, the Lord of preservation, tells Yudhisthira, this is a war that must be won. And if a lie needs ought to be told to win it, then a lie must be told. Krishna knows Drona's only weakness is his son Ashwathama. So, he asks Yudhisthira to spread the word that Ashwathama is dead. But Yudhisthira's morality and reputation will not permit him to lie. He despises dishonesty.

Even as Yudhisthira is thinking through Krishna's proposition and its implications, Bhima, one of the Pandava brothers, kills an elephant named Ashwathama and screams: "Ashwathama is dead." Word reaches Drona, and he thinks it is his son that Bhima has killed. He is stunned but refuses to believe the news until he hears it directly from Yudhisthira. He summons his student to his camp.

With Krishna's words still ringing in his ears, Yudhisthira stands in front of Drona.

"Is it true," Drona asks him, "Ashwathama is dead?"

"Yes," replies Yudhisthira, his voice trailing off inaudibly, "Ashwathama, the elephant."

Technically, Yudhisthira did not lie. But Drona doesn't hear the word elephant, so he lays down his weapons and bows his head in grief. In that very instant, on Krishna's instructions, Dhrishtadyumna, Yudhisthira's brother-in-law, chops Drona's head off.

In Vedic society, this is the worst possible crime. On the back of subterfuge, the Pandavas killed Drona, an unarmed Brahmin who had been a Guru to them in their younger days. It had to be done for the sake of "dharma," Krishna argued. But even today, we still question that wisdom. Was it really "dharma" – the path of rightness – to lie in order to kill?

I often pondered on this story and the fact that half a truth is often a great lie. Particularly as a half-truth was waiting for me that, in time, would turn my world upside down.

On October 22, 1989, during my industrial placement year working for a telecoms company, Sia and I got engaged. And although it's probably one of the most overused clichés in the world, I can honestly say it was the happiest day of my life. That I had made the first official step towards spending the rest of my life with this remarkable and beautiful woman set my heart dancing like summer rain. There must have been at least 200 guests at our engagement ceremony, but the only face I wanted to see was Sia's. As I waited for her to make her entrance, every passing minute seemed like an eternity. I was distracted by friends and relatives greeting and congratulating me, so when I next managed to look up, she was already there, standing on the stage like a vision from my dreams. If I had the power to stop time, I would have stopped it right there. I wanted to stay in that moment forever – for a thousand years at least - mesmerized by her beauty and perfection. I felt so blessed that the gods from high heaven had sent her down to me.

She looked stunning. Her skin glowed as though lit from the inside, her hair was swept up into a Japanese style bun, and her pink-purple sari complemented the natural flush staining her lips and cheeks. I could see she was nervous by the way she clenched her fists and the way her eyes darted around the room, reminding me of a frightened little bird. As soon as she caught sight of me, her lips curled into a smile, and she visibly relaxed. It was a magical moment. Our love for each other was tangible. It filled every space in my heart and spilled out of me, seeming to scent the air with the most beautiful, sweet fragrance. Our eyes locked. It was just the two of us. No one else in the world existed until one of the aunties broke the spell by interrupting our moment to ask Sia a question. But as soon as the auntie left her side, Sia's eyes sought mine again, then lowered to the floor in a show of endearing shyness.

I knew she was the ideal woman for me. She would be the most perfect wife and companion. We were engaged now. She was officially mine, and my world was complete.

The following day was Sia's 21st birthday, and I happily blew my overdraft limit, savings, and entire wages on spoiling her. Nothing was off-limits, and she returned home that day loaded up with shopping bags full of new clothes and extra special treats. Sia was keen for us to get married as soon as possible, but as my older brother was planning to marry his girlfriend, too, Mum and Dad insisted that his wedding should take place first. It was frustrating, but I used the extra year wisely, extending my industrial placement to two years instead of one and saving up like crazy so I could give Sia the wedding and the honeymoon of her dreams.

In the meantime, we managed to snatch some glorious weekends away together. Sia would tell her parents she was attending a company course when she was actually snuggled up beside me in a countryside hotel or a seaside B&B. We made the most of these precious times together, cherishing the snatched hours and nights, and getting to know each other intimately. Sia's lips were sweet for mine, and I didn't mind that she lied to her parents as she did it because she loved me and wanted us to be close.

On Sunday 11 August 1991, exactly a week after my brother's wedding, the day I had been dreaming about finally arrived. I was about to be joined in holy matrimony to the most perfect woman, to live in harmony and happiness forever. For once in my life, my confidence was at an all-time high. Knowing that Sia was mine and would be by my side forever made me feel like I could conquer the world. I felt so strong and proud and deliriously happy that the day had come that would mark the beginning of our new life together as husband and wife.

My wedding outfit was gold silk shot through with green and garnered plenty of compliments from the moment I left home in a long convoy of cars full of excited friends and relatives. When we arrived at the marriage hall, I was warmly received by the women of Sia's family while her brothers stood waiting in the background. I grinned at her twin brother, who I had grown particularly close to, and I was filled with brotherly love for him, knowing that he was now part of my family.

Sia's adoptive parents graciously washed my feet as part of the Hindu ceremony, while the ladies from my side of the family sat behind me, taunting my in-laws with gentle tongue-in-cheek songs. As my in-laws replied in turn with teasing words of their own, the lyrics became funnier and funnier. They warned their daughter that her new husband was useless and no good, while my family replied by singing that I was in trouble and trapped because I was marrying their daughter. It was all done in good humour and brought smiles to everyone's faces, but if I had known how prophetic their words would turn out to be in years to come, joy would have fled my heart, and my bones would have chilled to the marrow.

I sat behind a veil to prevent me from setting eyes on my loved one as she entered the stage and sat opposite me, placing the palm of her hand face down on the palm of my upturned hand. The most beautiful mehndi of intricate design adorned her wrists, hands, and fingers. Stunning floral patterns, trailed patterns, criss-cross details, vines, and even an exquisite peacock had been drawn onto her skin in henna by a skilled and practiced hand. Traditionally, it is said that the darker the stain of the mehndi, the more love the bride will receive from her husband and in-laws. At that moment, I knew that she had all the love I could possibly give to anyone. No one could have loved her more. I smiled to myself, remembering the other tradition that said brides should abstain from doing any housework until the henna stain on their hands fades away.

The sound of the spiritual mantras echoed around us – beautiful, soothing, uplifting, and timeless. Then the moment came for the veil to be removed, and there in front of me, sat the breathtaking vision of the woman I had loved and adored for the past three years. She looked more beautiful than ever in her red and white wedding sari; the only thing missing was her mesmerizing smile. I put this down to nerves. After all, it was the most important day of our lives to date, and we were determined for it to be perfect.

Her missing smile cast a shadow across my heart and planted a dark seed of secret anguish in my mind. Only five days before our wedding, Sia had told me she had missed a period. She was desperately worried in case anyone found out, as in the Gujarati community, it is taboo and deeply shameful to have sex before marriage. I tried to reassure her, telling her everything would be fine, not to worry, and to focus instead on our special day.

The day after our wedding, a doctor confirmed Sia's pregnancy and, at a later appointment, gave us an expected due date. Now, I had never been an enthusiastic maths student, but I was pretty good at basic arithmetic, so when I began working backward from the due date given, I was puzzled. The numbers didn't add up. Or, at least, something didn't add up. I tried not to dwell on it too much as we had our honeymoon to look forward to, as well as a joint post-wedding event with my newlywed brother. It was supposed to be a happy occasion for everyone, but I found myself fixated on dates. I couldn't talk to anyone about my concerns, least of all Sia. I was alone with my dark thoughts, and I was terrified of what they might lead to.

Sitting on the plane on our way to spend the six weeks of our honeymoon in India, Malaysia, and Singapore, I thought about the three and a half years leading up to our wedding. Those years had been the happiest times of my life. I was totally lost in my love for Sia. Being with her had eradicated my heartache at being forced to study subjects that were against my nature. She had changed my life for the better. She had set me on a joyous pathway to the future. She had given me confidence in myself and my abilities and the thought that any of this might be threatened was too unbearable to contemplate.

We had planned to spend three days in Delhi, two in Agra, and two more in Jaipur before heading back to Delhi. But the monsoons that season were late, and the country was engulfed in a heat wave, that even by Indian standards, was intense. Daytime temperatures reached over 40 degrees. It was sticky and humid, and in the early stages of pregnancy, Sia found it unbearable. Consequently, we changed our plans and cancelled our trip to Jaipur.

My new wife was behaving very differently from the sweet-natured girl she had been before our wedding: the girl who had melted my heart and showered me in loving kisses.

Her smile was nowhere to be seen, and her manner towards me altered from gentle and tender to impatient and sharp. I tried to put this change down to the heat and her rampaging hormones, but even so, suddenly, I felt as though I didn't know her anymore. Despite all of this, I tried my best not to dwell on the disquieting thoughts that hovered menacingly at the edges of my mind and tried instead to concentrate on having a wonderful and memorable honeymoon.

The highlight of our trip to Agra was, of course, one of the great wonders of the world - the Taj Mahal. Both Sia and I were astounded by the beauty of this world-famous monument, built from white marble etched with intricate calligraphy and inlaid with gemstones. The gardens surrounding it were equally as breath taking, and we stood in silence for a while in pure contemplation of its magnificence. The love story behind its construction was mesmerizing, and we listened attentively as our guide told us all about Mughal emperor Shah Jahan and his beloved wife, Mumtaz Mahal.

The legendary couple met in 1607, before Shah Jahan, grandson of Akbar the Great, became the fifth emperor of the Mughal Empire. It was love at first sight, but as tradition dictated, the two were not allowed to marry straight away as Shah Jahan had to take another wife. Eventually, five years after they had first met, the love-struck couple married, and Shah Jahna bestowed on his new wife the name, Mumtaz

Mahal, meaning, 'chosen one of the palace.'

Mumtaz Mahal, was by all accounts as beautiful as she was intelligent and kind-hearted. The people took her to their hearts, not least because she cared for them, ensuring that widows and orphans were looked after and given food and money. Mumtaz Mahal gave birth to fourteen children, of which only seven survived beyond infancy. It was the birth of her fourteenth child that led to her untimely death.

Mumtaz Mahal always accompanied her husband on his military campaigns, despite being heavily pregnant. During one such campaign just three years into Shah Jahan's reign, she went into labour and gave birth to a healthy baby girl inside a royal tent in the middle of the army encampment. All seemed well at first, but then Mumtaz Mahal fell ill and died in her husband's arms the very next day.

Shah Jahan was beyond distraught. He shut himself away in his tent and wept non-stop for eight days. It was said that when he finally emerged, his hair had turned white. When he returned to Agra, he poured his grief into designing and building the most elaborate and expensive mausoleum the world had ever seen and the first to be dedicated to a woman. With plenty of riches at his disposal, Shah Jahan let his imagination and ambition run riot. Over twenty thousand workers and over a thousand elephants were employed to build the exquisite monument, which took twenty-two years to complete. Upon his death, Shah Jahan was buried with his soul mate, his favourite wife, Mumtaz Mahal, in the crypt beneath the Taj Mahal - united for all eternity.

As our guide pointed towards the chambers where Shah Jahan and his wife were entombed, my own wife let out a loud belch and vomited right in front of the most beautiful building in the world. The sickness that plagued her during the early weeks of her pregnancy, combined with the heat of the day, had quite overcome her. The tour guide scowled at us, throwing us such a look of disgust anyone would have thought we had committed the most heinous of crimes. As I helped Sia over to a bench to recover, I flashed the tour guide a beaming smile, thinking how, in comparison to Sia's beauty, it was a fitting reply to Mumtaz's beauty.

The next part of our trip took us to Malaysia, with its stunning beaches, abundant rainforests, and over eight hundred tiny islands. The flight was long, bumpy, and arduous and as soon as we landed and disembarked, Sia, feeling very unwell, had to rush to the nearest bathroom. By the time she had recovered somewhat and emerged, the other passengers had all disappeared from view. The airport was undergoing some major renovations at the time, so the signage had been removed. As there were no other passengers around for us to follow, we became confused about which way to go. There was no inquiry desk and no officials to ask. We wandered around for a while, unable to locate the international arrivals exit until finally, we found a man who spoke a little English who pointed us in the direction of the domestic exit. Thinking we would be told where to go, we approached with our passports at the ready. To my surprise, the border control officer showed no interest in our passports and waved us straight through. This didn't feel quite right, but I just assumed it was how things were done in Malaysia.

The following day we travelled by taxi to the island of Penang – the food capital of Malaysia and The Pearl of the Orient. To our horror and bewilderment, when we tried to exchange some money at our hotel, the manager called the police, who proceeded to escort us to the local police station, where we were detained for over six hours. All because we didn't have Malaysian arrival stamps on our passports.

It was a highly unpleasant experience. We tried our best to explain that we had made a mistake at the airport in exiting via domestic arrivals instead of international arrivals. But it hadn't been our fault, and no one had checked. We explained ourselves over and over again, but it seemed all the Chief of Police was interested in was yelling down the phone at someone asking why we had no stamp. Despite explaining that my wife was pregnant and unwell, the police refused our requests for water and insisted on keeping Sia detained alongside me. In the end, the British Consulate got involved, and we were finally released without charge.

Luckily, the rest of our stay in Penang was much less

dramatic. Our hotel was fabulous, and for the next six days, we took full advantage of the luxury pool, the soft, sandy beach out in front, and the endless choice of fresh fruit juices on offer from the hotel bar (although the much lauded starfruit juice got the thumbs down from both of us). Finally, Sia's gorgeous smile returned to her face, and I dared to believe the honeymoon of our dreams was finally happening.

From Penang, we travelled 50km north of Kuala Lumpur to the mist-cloaked heights of Genting Highlands and the glitz and glamour of Resorts World. We explored the vast entertainment complex for the next couple of days, with its malls, amusement parks, bars, casinos, and all the cool, fresh mountain air we could wish for.

However much I tried to put it to the back of my mind, I couldn't shake off my unease regarding the delivery date of our child. The frantic calculations and counting of weeks and dates kept clicking through my brain. The nasty seed that had planted itself in my mind was growing damaging, invasive roots, and I didn't even have the courage to mention my doubts to Sia. My suspicions were eating away at my insides, torturing me, and threatening my happiness. One night, back at our hotel, I couldn't get the dark thoughts out of my mind. It was impossible to sleep, so leaving Sia snoring gently in our bed, I crept out of our room and made my way to a casino.

It was gone midnight by the time I walked into the razzle-dazzle world of roulette, poker, baccarat, and black jack. The crowded, glittering room was a far cry from my usual habitat; in fact, it was the first time I had ever frequented a casino. But I had been desperate to get away for a while; to be on my own to contemplate the matters that had been bugging me since our wedding day. I had 25 Malaysian dollars to play with – the equivalent of £5 sterling. I amused myself for the next few hours, placing a bet here and a bet there, losing some and winning some. It was soothing, and somehow being in that place, with all the noise, bright lights, and chatter of other people, distracted me from my concerns and made me feel better than I had done the whole honeymoon. Before I knew it, the sun had risen, and it was 8 a.m. I crept back to our hotel room, imagining Sia to be still sleeping. But when I opened the door, she was sitting up in bed wide awake and worried to death. She had woken five hours earlier with no idea of where I was. And me, being the idiot, hadn't thought to leave a note to let her know where I was. Not that I could have told her that my worries over our child's due date had prevented me from sleeping. Needless to say, Mr Kotecha received his first lecture from Mrs Kotetcha that morning.

We spent the last two weeks of our honeymoon in Mumbai, and by this time, I had managed to convince myself that the doctor had made a mistake in his calculations or that the due date he had given was only an approximation. In any case, I banished all negative thoughts from my mind and instead took Sia shopping for new saris and Punjabi dresses. She must have been amazed by my generosity, but little did she know that I had soon realized, in true Gujarati style, that all these things were a fraction of the price compared to what they would cost me in London. I only hoped she would not ask for any more new outfits for a good while to come.

EIGHT

"Be the change that you wish to see in the world."

-   *Mahatma Gandhi*

The night before we left Vadodara to travel to Rajkot for the next stage of our trip, I decided it was high time Papa Bear, Mummy Bear, and Baby Bear went out for some proper porridge. We had consumed enough junk food over the last few days; our bodies deserved some nutritional pampering. We booked a table at Mandap -The Authentic Gujarati Thali Restaurant, which came highly recommended by the Bank of Baroda manager. Quite often in India, if a place is recommended, there is a commission, family favour, or other incentive involved. That was not the case with this particular restaurant. Along with its mouthful of a name, this place served mouthfuls of the most exquisite vegetarian delights.

Situated on the first floor of the Hotel Express Towers, the Mandap specialised in a particular style of eating in India known as Thali, from the Hindi word meaning large plate or platter. Thali, the meal, however, refers to many different dishes served in small bowls arranged on a platter (Thali). The Mandap was famous for its constantly flowing, eat all-you-like style Thali, which meant we were able to sample a huge range of tastes and flavours, all of them out-of-this-world delicious. I counted at least five curries: bhindi masala, bateta nu shaak with thick gravy, ful-gobi matar nu shaak, akha ringna bateta nu shaak, and tindola nu shaak. These were accompanied by plain rice, jeera rice, mixed vegetable pilau rice, and a variety of hot chapatti breads, from rotis, puris, parathas, aloo parathas, pooran puris, to others I didn't even know the name of. And if that wasn't enough, there was a vast selection of savouries, too: samosas, patras, bhajias, plain poppadoms, spicy masala poppadoms, and my favourite, khandvi. All this came with unlimited Gujarati style lassi known as chaas, fried green chillis, salad, and achar.

Papa was in heaven when the sweets came out. Despite the amount of food we had already put away, he had to try every single one: Gulab jambus, kheer, and gajar no halvo with ice cream. And with every mouthful, he rolled his eyes in ecstasy and smacked his lips with relish. We had saved ourselves all day for this culinary experience and hadn't eaten since breakfast. I am sure the amount of food we managed to polish off must have left the restaurant manager quaking in his boots. It had been a feast for the eyes, stomach, and soul.

We emerged from the Mandap, happy, satisfied, stuffed to the gills, and barely able to walk. We were due to catch the overnight luxury sleeper bus at 1.30 am to take us to Rajkot, and as we had a few hours to wait, I suggested we booked into a hotel room so Mum and Dad could get some sleep. They wouldn't hear of it. Why waste money on a hotel room when there were perfectly good cinema seats available? So, with all our luggage in tow, we headed to the nearest cinema, and for the third time in four nights, we settled down to watch the late night movie, Chal Jivi Live. I was sure Mum and Dad would nod off, so I booked the higher priced luxury seats so at least they could snore in comfort. As usual, they confounded me and stayed awake throughout the whole film. Maybe, I should have booked the cheaper seats after all!

Even though we had seen Chal Jivi Live a couple of times already, the power of its story and its deeper message affected us just as much. There were plenty of tears rolling down our cheeks, and I believe that subconsciously, the movie impacted our thinking for the rest of the trip, making us hyper-aware of the importance of making the most of our lives together, as who knows how long we would have?

India's luxury Volvo sleeper buses are most definitely the most convenient way to travel. I was wise enough to book our tickets well in advance. It is common knowledge that drivers often make extra cash by picking up extra customers on the highway and stashing them in unreserved seats or even in the driver's cockpit. But aside from this, the buses themselves were double-decked and boasted six feet long double beds on the left and single beds on the right, complete with Wi-Fi, power sockets, personal TV screens, and thick curtains for privacy. Fresh pillows, sheets, and blankets were also provided.

We were all exhausted by now, so we gratefully climbed into our beds and settled down for the night, quickly realising that loud snoring from multiple directions was to be our sound track for the journey.

Just after 7 am, and two hours from Rajkot, the driver pulled into a service station so we could all stretch our legs and grab some breakfast. We didn't have to be persuaded to eat, of course, and proceeded to wash down a delicious junkie feast of vada pau, fafra ganthis and fried green chillies with big gulps of masala tea.

When I visited the toilets, I was shocked and pleasantly surprised to find they were more or less comparable to the bathrooms in any British motorway service station. It was such a pleasure not to have the usual stench attacking my nostrils. I was glad to see progress was, at long last, being made in that area. Sanitation has long been an issue in India. The government and Prime Minister Narendra Modi have been fighting to end open defecation for years, installing eighteen million new toilets across the country and allocating funds for villages to build their own sewage systems and lavatories.

It had been a huge and continuing challenge to try and change villagers' attitudes towards defecating in open fields. Because of India's lack of sanitation infrastructure, the practice became a deeply entrenched part of their culture. For some people, defecating outside was an opportunity to socialise, an enjoyable activity that complied with spiritual and religious norms. Even with access to a toilet at home, some women continued to defecate in the open due to privacy issues, the thought of being confined in a small space, or the fact that some toilets were reserved for the exclusive use of men. Plus, many people still believed building toilets inside homes – where washing, cooking, and worship took place – was simply dirty.

After years of training themselves to withhold their natural bodily functions during the daytime, many women would wait until nightfall before heading out to a dark field or wooded area to relieve themselves and were consequently at risk of attack, rape, and abuse. In some places, the incident of rape was on the rise, yet the village elders still refused to have toilets installed. It was becoming an increasingly dangerous practice, and I also often wondered how a woman managed if she had an upset stomach or injured her foot or leg and couldn't walk to the fields.

Amazingly, Toilet Ek Prem Katha, a Bollywood movie, has made great strides in changing villager's attitudes. It's a simple plot telling the true story of a woman who leaves her husband very early in their marriage after discovering he doesn't have a toilet in his house. The husband sets out on a desperate mission to win his wife back by standing up to and going against India's long-established traditions and values and finally installing modern sanitation. The filmmaker hoped that bringing the issue of open defecation to the silver screen would inspire people to tackle the on-going problem that has blighted so many lives and deprived women of their privacy, safety, and dignity for far too long. I was glad to see the fight was finally succeeding, and I was eternally grateful that Mum had never had to face such dangers and humiliation.

By 10 am we were in the heart of the bustling city of Rajkot. The last major city in Gujarat before heading into the rural depths of Saurastra, Rajkot is rated in the top ten of the cleanest cities in India and was home to Mahatma Gandhi for a portion of his childhood. It is a beautiful place, rich in history and culture, and famous for its sweets, silk works, gold jewellery, and watches. It is a city perfect for lovers of food and shopping.

We were lucky enough to have family here, a very dear cousin named Vishal (his maternal grandmother and my paternal grandfather were siblings) who had kindly offered rooms in his house for us to stay. For the rest of our time in India, we planned to use Vishal's place as a base and somewhere to leave the main bulk of our luggage while we travelled elsewhere.

As we settled into our rooms, unpacked our bags, and rested awhile to recover from the long coach trip, I heard the sound of Mum and Dad's raised voices coming from behind their closed door. They had obviously already forgotten they were on holiday, and it saddened me to hear them replaying the same old arguments they had been having for years. I could only imagine what Vishal must have been thinking as Mum and Dad's bickering became louder and louder and could surely be heard all the way downstairs. The same old subject reared its head again, transporting me back to my college days in the mid-eighties when Dad had a short affair with a woman for which Mum had never forgiven him.

I remembered how badly the revelation affected me at the time. It dealt a massive blow to my confidence, and I had no idea how to handle it all. I would lock myself up in my room to cry alone, and I would skip lessons at college to hide away in the corner of the refectory instead. I was so angry at Dad, but I was angry at the woman, too. How dare she ruin my happy family! I was so scared of what might happen to us all. But then, at that age, I was frightened and resentful of a lot of stuff. Particularly my big, bossy brother, who had made me go to college and study a subject I had little interest or enthusiasm for.

Even in my adulthood, I still harboured resentment towards the woman Dad had his fling with. She reminded me - or at least her character reminded me - all too viscerally and painfully of how I had been betrayed and hurt by Sia and how the fallout from that betrayal had passed down another generation.

NINE

"Strength is Life, Weakness is Death. Expansion is Life, Contraction is Death. Love is Life, Hatred is Death."

-    *Swami Vivekananda*

W hen I first met Sia, I had no idea of the sort of life she had led or the traumas she had suffered as a child. When she finally confided in me and told me the story of her childhood, my personal hang-ups paled into insignificance. For what could be worse for a child than seeing your mother murdered right in front of your very eyes?

Sia's mother was called Chanderika Tanna. She had been forced into an early marriage to the son of Daya Lal Tanna. It was not a happy match, although three children were born from the union, the eldest being Sia and her twin brother, and a younger sister. Chanderika grew ever more unhappy in her marriage and began searching for love and affection elsewhere. Against the traditions of her culture and the sanctity of marriage, she sought out other men and embarked on numerous affairs. She was never particularly discreet and living in a close-knit community, her dishonourable behaviour was soon noted.

Rumours abounded. The worst being that Chanderika was not only indulging in sex outside marriage with other men but that she had taken part in a threesome. The earliest Gujarati threesome in the UK, as it came to be described by Chandulal Thakrar, a close relative. Shame rained down on her family by the bucket full. But even when she was challenged and asked to stop, Chanderika remained unrepentant.

One fateful day in April 1974, Chanderika was preparing to leave the house to meet one of her lovers. Her father-in-law, Daya Lal Tanna, had by this time grown sickened by her behaviour and the shame she was heaping upon the family. He confronted her in the kitchen of her home and tried to prevent her from leaving. He begged her to stop seeing other men, change her behaviour, be a faithful wife, and set a moral standard for her children. But Chanderika was having none of it. She pushed past Daya Lal Tanna and swore at him, telling him to mind his own business.

Daya Lal Tanna became enraged. He picked up a knife from the kitchen and followed Chanderika into the back garden. And there, in front of five-year-old Sia and Chanderika's two other young children, he attacked her and stabbed her to death.

Daya Lal Tanna was later arrested, charged, and convicted of murder. But he maintained that in the Hindu faith, if a woman has sex outside marriage or with a stranger, it is not a sin to kill her, even if the killing is a crime in the eyes of the law. He expressed no regrets, saying that, yes, he stabbed Chanderika with the full intention of killing her.

Daya Lal Tanna's act of violence and the taking of human life cannot be condoned in any way, shape, or form. He committed an act of murder, and for that, he deserved his punishment. The legacy of his actions brought shame upon his entire family and the Gujarati community. The shame was so great that the family was forced to move away to Milton Keynes, to a place where there were no Gujarati families, and they could live in obscurity.

The murder devastated an entire generation, and its effects continue to ripple down the years. As a child, Sia was understandably traumatised to have witnessed her mother die in such a brutal fashion. The whole family was ripped apart. Sia's father went mad with grief and was committed to a psychiatric unit, while Sia and her two siblings were sent to live with her father's brother and his wife.

The wife, Sia's auntie, greatly resented this arrangement as she already had three children in the house. As a consequence, she treated Sia and her siblings as outsiders. Akin to a modern-day Cinderella story, they were forced to do all the housework before they went to school, sent out in the cold without coats, and made to bathe in cold water. They were also denied the university education granted to their cousins and were instead sent out to work as soon as they turned sixteen.

That Sia had a terrible and traumatic childhood cannot be denied. But I couldn't help thinking that surely her mother should be made accountable for some of the terrible things that were wrought on the family? Had she learned to keep her lust for other men at bay and put the needs of her children first, then how different things could have turned out. How different things could have been for the entire family.

If Chanderika had put her family above her desires, her children would have had a mother to love them and teach them moral standards. They would have had a grandfather in their lives instead of in prison. A grandfather to love them and for them to love back. And the family would never have had to hide their faces in shame.

The more I thought about it, the more I realised that the way Chanderika had lived her life, her deep attachment to sex, and her compulsion to chase after love from one man to another had destroyed her daughters' morals and indirectly taught them that lust, feelings of inadequacies, and openly sleeping around were acceptable ways to live a life. In my mind, Chanderika had never been a true mother. How could she have been? It seemed to me she had given birth to her children, but she had never given them life. A true mother protects her children and teaches them to live righteous lives. A true mother's children should be born out of a solid, committed union and not from short-lived sexual gratification. And a true mother would not abandon her children to chase after other men.

Parents are living Gods to their children, and they should uphold this position. By seeking out sexual gratification outside of her marriage, Chanderika had placed her needs above those of her offspring, and the results were devastating and far-reaching.

I learned just how far-reaching a few years into my marriage, when I discovered that Sia had followed in her mother's footsteps by indulging in numerous affairs. Throughout our marriage, Sia had sought to protect her mother's honour and character by portraying her as an innocent victim of a murdering rapist, drunk grandfather. To Sia, her mother was a hero, and the fact that she slept around was conveniently airbrushed from family history. But the truth of the past cannot be escaped, and the tragedy that had befallen her mother left Sia incapable of loving herself or accepting love from others, including me. I had my suspicions for a while, but all my questions and accusations only drove Sia further into the arms of other men and culminated in her eventually leaving me for a married man and taking our children with her, maybe hoping he would leave his wife and children. Our daughter had been born eight months after our Indian marriage ceremony, and our son followed five years later. What had happened to the girl I had fallen in love with? The wonderful sweet woman I had given my heart and soul to? The perfect woman I had thought was mine forever.

I was left bereft and scared; my dreams shattered, my marriage in tatters, and my children torn from my arms and my heart. The misgivings that had haunted me since our wedding day came back with a vengeance. If Sia was unfaithful to me now, had she been cheating from the very beginning? Had I been right to question the due date of our first child? My precious, precious daughter. No matter how hard I tried, I couldn't rid myself of the questions and doubts that crowded my mind every second of every day.

Finally, I broke and ordered a DNA test. With a single hair from my daughter's head and a single hair from mine, my future and my family's future would be determined. The wait for results was agonising. When the letter arrived, I held it in my hand, turning it over and over, too afraid to slit open the envelope. Too afraid to confront the truth. But eventually, I summoned up the courage, and just as my finger sliced through the envelope seal, tearing the paper jaggedly apart, the words I read inside sliced through my heart and tore it to shreds. At that moment, my world changed forever.

My daughter was not mine.

For thirteen years, we had lived a lie.

TEN

"Honor thy Mother as God. Honor thy Father as God. Honor thy Teacher as God. Honor thy Guest as God."

- *Shijshavalli I 11.2 in Taittriya Upanishad*

I tried not to let past traumas intrude too much into the present, as I didn't want anything to spoil Mum and Dad's trip. So far, everything had gone to plan. We enjoyed India's very best, from its food, culture, architecture, and stunning scenery to the famous Indian attitude of treating guests as Gods. We had been welcomed everywhere with open arms and unparalleled hospitality. Atithi Devo Bhavah (the guest is equivalent to god) is integral to the Indian way of life. It is a Sanskrit verse taken from Hindu scriptures and has become part of the code of conduct for Hindu society. This intrinsic part of Indian culture is one of the main reasons the British took advantage of India. They came to trade, were welcomed as guests and treated as Gods, and then took over the country!

The next planned stop-off on our busy itinerary was to a

place very dear to Dad and somewhere he was very excited to be going. Leaving the majority of our luggage at 'base camp,' we travelled south from Rajkot to the village of Kodinar where one of Dad's paternal aunties had lived. The city held a special place in Dad's heart, as it was steeped in family history and memories. En route, we stopped at the village of Laduli in the southern part of Gir forest, the birthplace of Dad's father. We didn't stay for long as we knew we would be returning for a more in-depth visit later in our trip. It was from Laduli that Dad's parents had immigrated to Africa, with family lore telling the tale of how my grandfather had been gently coaxed into leaving India. So the story goes, my grandmother's two brothers were immigrating to Africa and had persuaded my grandfather to take them to Bombay so their sister (my grandmother) could wave them off. Once they arrived in Bombay, the two brothers told my grandfather that as he had come as far as Bombay, he might as well carry on to Africa, as the economic situation there was much better than in India. When grandfather protested, citing the fact that he and my grandmother didn't have passports, or the money to travel, the two brothers brushed away the excuse. They offered to pay the travelling costs, and took my grandfather straight to the passport office where they just happened to know a guy who could help. In those days, with India still a British Colony, getting hold of a passport was no big deal. "Just come with us to see what you think," the two brothers said. "If you don't like it, you can always come back."

My grandfather never did go back to India, and sadly, because he died when my father was only eight years old, the two sisters he left behind never got to see him again. A fact which the oldest of the aunties never forgave my grandmother for – blaming her for letting her two brothers persuade my grandfather into immigrating to Africa in the first place!

Years later, Dad travelled to India to visit the two aunties, one in Malia and one in Kodinar. They were overwhelmed to see him and became very close. He visited again in 1967, bringing Mum, and my brother, and me with him. I was only two and a quarter at the time, so I have no memory of this trip; I only know it was in Kodinar that I was given my first haircut as part of the Mundan Ceremonial Ritual. In Hinduism, the mundan is one of sixteen purification rituals known as Shodasha Samskara. According to Hindu mythology, a soul only acquires a human body after experiencing eighty-four lakh yonis. Every yoni leaves its influence on human birth, and the shaving of the child's head is believed to rid the child of any negativity from their past life. It is a gesture of purification from previous yonis and brings freedom from the past. The shaving of the head is also believed to promote spiritual and mental development. Even though I can't remember my own Mundan Ceremony, I have always been proud that it was conducted in a place so dear and full of meaning to Dad.

Dad was thrilled to be in Kodinar again and to be reunited with his auntie's youngest son. Years before, Dad had given this auntie and her older sister an equal sum of money each. The money had gone towards medical treatments for one sister, and the other sister had used the money to start a business. Neither of them had ever forgotten Dad's kindness and generosity towards them. Unfortunately, although the business had been a huge success at first, with my youngest auntie's eldest son becoming involved, it was challenging to run an independent business in the 1980s. Everyone was out for a share of the profits, including the police and other officials. My cousin unwisely chose to become involved in the black market, mixing with and dealing with people he should have steered clear of. The business collapsed, and he ended up owing a lot of money to these unsavoury characters. Like a scene from an action movie, the unsavoury characters kidnapped my uncle's younger son, Lalo, in a dramatic turn of events. They held him as ransom, threatening to kill not only him but the entire family if the money owed was not paid back.

Luckily no murders were committed, but my uncle remained a wanted man and had to escape from the village in the dead of night, finally settling down in a place best not mentioned in this book. Dad's youngest cousin, Jitendra (who stayed in the village as he had done nothing wrong), vowed to walk barefoot in the act of penance for his older brother. He was true to his word, and when I met him on a previous visit to India, I mistook him for a vagrant, with his blackened feet and overgrown beard. This time around, he was back to his usual self and was even wearing a pair of shoes

Jitendra, or Jitu kaka, as I fondly called him, had arranged for us to stay at a friend's house. Knowing my aversion to anything other than a western style toilet, he had thoughtfully and cleverly anticipated my needs, and his friend had kindly given over the top floor of his house to us – complete with western style toilet, of course. We enjoyed a fantastic first evening, and my auntie treated us to the most incredible meal. She was one of those intuitive cooks who make the process of cooking seem so effortless. Without using recipe books, weights, or measurements, she chatted away as she threw a pinch of spice here and there, stirred and chopped and tasted before conjuring up, as if by magic, at least ten dishes of sublime deliciousness. Dad was in his element, catching up on family news, reminiscing, laughing, joking, and generally revelling in being surrounded by his loving family in a place that meant so much to him.

Later that evening, after returning to our rooms at Jitu kaka's friend's house, Mum brought up the subject of my brother and my divorce. As much as I tried to bite my tongue, and as much as I asked Mum to bite her tongue, she wouldn't change the subject, and before we knew it, old wounds had opened, and the conversation became heated.

ELEVEN

There isn't a tree in the world that the wind hasn't shaken.

- *Hindu Proverb*

If I thought finding out my daughter was another man's child was the most devastating thing that could ever happen to me, I was sadly mistaken. The day I received the DNA test results was the worst of my life, without a doubt, but what followed almost destroyed me. The lies and betrayals piled up thick and fast, and the truth was twisted and distorted until it was barely recognisable.

Understandably, when I first suspected Sia of being unfaithful to me, I was angry. Who wouldn't be? Part of me couldn't believe she would ever do something like that. She was such a wonderful woman in so many ways. Her good qualities shone out of her brighter than almost any other person I knew. But the evidence against her was stacking up. And the more I confronted her, and the more I voiced my suspicions, the more I pushed her into the arms of other men. It was a vicious cycle that I didn't have the power to break.

Sia's brother told me I was suffering from paranoia and advised me to see a psychiatrist to help save my marriage. I was so desperate, I agreed. But the problem wasn't in my head, and the medication prescribed for my anxiety only plunged me further into depression. Little did I know that the suggestion to see a psychiatrist was not out of concern for my wellbeing. In time to come, during my divorce proceedings, the very fact I had visited a psychiatrist was held against me in court as evidence of my mental instability.

Once we were living apart, I continued to see my kids every two weeks. They were the lights of my life, and I tried to make the most of every second spent with them. But I still could not shake off the suspicions that had haunted me since my wedding day. Was I truly my daughter's biological father? I decided to finally put my mind at rest by sending a sample of my daughter's hair and mine to be tested.

When the DNA results came through confirming my suspicions, on the same day as my decree absolute, my entire world shattered into tiny pieces. It was no comfort to know I had been right all along to be distrustful of my wife's behaviour, and there had never been a need to see a psychiatrist due to my supposed paranoia.

But the knowledge that my wife had been unfaithful to me only weeks before our wedding, that another man's child had been growing in her belly as we walked around the sacred flames during our Hindu fire ceremony, and that she had continued to be unfaithful throughout our marriage, severely affected my state of my mind. How could it not? Anger mixed with battered self-confidence and a loss of self-respect was a lethal combination.

But what I didn't expect was for my own brother to twist the knife or for Sia's family to twist the knife. It seemed the whole world was against me when all I had done was love my wife and children unconditionally and faithfully. I realised too late that Sia had followed in her mother's footsteps. Like every child, she had learned the lessons taught to her.

If I had thought the divorce was horrendous, worse was yet to come. When I told Sia I knew the truth and had the DNA results to prove it, she refused to let me see the children again and proceeded to fill their heads with lies about me. Fingers were pointed my way. For everything Sia had done to destroy our marriage, I was now the accused. I was now the villain. She accused me of faking the DNA results, and her brother threatened to sue me for defamation if I exposed the truth of his biological mother's and two sisters' adulterous behaviour. Years later, even my own daughter lied in the witness box to protect her mother and only undisputed parent after realising I was telling the truth about the DNA test. And finally, even my son turned against me and refused to see me anymore.

I was a broken man. A shadow of myself with little

strength to fight the injustice of the whole process. I had given Sia whatever she needed financially, leaving myself only less than ten per cent of our combined wealth in the divorce settlement. I said yes to everything, and then I withdrew to take stock of the ruins of my life. I was a scared man, with the threat of being sued for defamation hanging over me, the heartbreak of my ex-wife's infidelity, and the knowledge that our whole marriage had been a lie. I realised, too, that because of the way my brother had always controlled me and pushed me into studying subjects I had no interest in, I had never had the chance to live the life *I* wanted.

All this changed when I signed up to participate in a seminar run by the respected and highly successful author and life coach, Tony Robbins. A pioneer in the industry, Tony has coached people from all walks of life, including the late Princess Diana. It was the best decision I ever made. That man totally transformed my life. He gave me back my strength and purpose, and made me realise that the only life worth living was one of truth. For too long, I had closed my eyes and ears to the truth, and so too, I realised, had the rest of my family – Mum in particular.

But no more, I vowed. From then on, I determined never to hide from the truth again. I would bring the truth into the light. The whole truth. I remembered, as it says in the tale of Drona, even half a truth is often a great lie.

After losing pretty much everything in the divorce, I moved in with Mum and Dad in their house in North London. It was an ideal arrangement. By then, they were both in their seventies and were happy to have me around to look after them. We didn't crowd each other out. They kept their independence, and I kept mine. But I was always on hand to sort out any problems or help with any computer related, business, or DIY issues. Plus, it gave them a sense of security to have me close by in case of an emergency or should an accident occur.

Unfortunately, my brother did not see it this way. Even though Dad had always been beyond generous towards his entire family and had already paid for over half of my brother's house, as well as insuring his children's university costs were all taken care of. For some reason, my brother was consumed with jealousy and anger. Maybe he thought that because I was living with Mum and Dad, I would get more than my fair share of Dad's money when the time came. But he was wrong. His fears were unfounded, as Dad had already written out his wishes, ensuring that everybody benefitted from his generosity equally.

But my brother's anger only grew. He couldn't take it out on me, as his five foot six inches height was no longer a match for my six foot three inches. Instead, he chose to take his anger, fear, and envy out on Dad. I never witnessed his violence myself, but I saw the pain in Dad's eyes, the bruises on his skin, and heard him crying as he prayed.

TWELVE

"Hope is a good thing. Maybe the best of things. And no good thing ever dies from it."

- *Shawshank Redemption*

"I hope, I pray, my truth finds my son."

- *Mayur Kotecha*

After practising what I learned through my coaching with Tony Robbins, I gradually regained some sense of my true self and found some healing from my divorce and the surrounding circumstances. With freshly buoyed confidence coursing through my veins, I decided to set myself a challenge. For nine years, I had determined to take part in the London Marathon, and finally, in 2015, I was selected to run on behalf of St. Luke's Hospice, a charity specialising in end of life and palliative care. I felt like a warrior heading into battle. Not only a physical battle to prepare myself for the challenge ahead, but in light of all that had happened in my life to date, a mental battle, too; a battle within myself, a war of thoughts running through my head.

I believed that Arjuna, son of the god Indra, was truly the sinless one, even on a battlefield. He didn't see warriors that he wanted to kill, only relatives and kinsmen who he loved deeply. I could relate to Arjuna's predictions of a difficult future ahead. No war is easy. No battle is easy, and I had to gather every ounce of courage in preparation to fight my own war, both on the ground and in my mind.

I threw myself wholeheartedly into training for the marathon, spending three solid months in the gym, running miles through the local streets, eating a healthy diet, including whey protein, and paying for sixteen one on one personal training sessions. Unfortunately, I never made it to my first training session. In early January 2016, a dear cousin fell critically ill and had only a short time to live. As soon as I heard the devastating news, all thoughts of training for the marathon flew from my mind.

I needed to be with my cousin, to do whatever I could to make her last days as happy and as comfortable as possible. So for the next three weeks, Mum, Dad, and I sat by her bedside in Leicester Royal Infirmary Hospital. We held her hand, gently stroked her brow, and reminded her how much we loved her. It was a tremendously sad time, as we tried to hold back our tears to concentrate on giving this wonderful human being the necessary strength to rest in peace. She had led a difficult and traumatic life, losing her mother when she was only two, suffering through a failed marriage, and most tragically of all, having to cremate one of her own children who died as a result of drug abuse. That she should now be dying before her time seemed impossibly unfair. It was utterly heart breaking. This brave lady's passing was so hard to bear, and many, many tears were shed at her funeral.

I was shattered by my cousin's death but found the best way to deal with my grief was to throw myself back into training for the marathon. Lili, my personal trainer, was worried I had left it too late. There wasn't enough time left to prepare my body for the stresses and strains of running twenty-six miles. I brushed her worries aside, believing that the strength of my determination was more than enough to overcome any physical failings. I doubled my visits to the gym and upped my hours spent running through the streets. My self-belief was at an all time high, my past traumas having finally taught me my true worth. By the third week of February, I could comfortably run five miles without becoming breathless. However, my calf and thigh muscles were not doing so well, so Lili suggested to strengthen my legs, I should incorporate hill climbing into my training regimen. I didn't need telling twice.

One of my favourite places in the world is the city of Rishikesh. It sits in the foothills of the Himalayas and is also known as the 'Gateway to the Garhwal Himalayas' and 'Yoga Capital of the World.' With no time to waste, I packed my bags and booked myself a stay in the Rishikesh Valley

Huts. Run by a couple called Anand and Subudi, this remote but luxurious and heavenly place lies between Rishikesh and Kunjapuri and is truly a feast for the senses. As far as the eye could see were lush trees and greenery and waterfalls. A small stream running behind my hut provided a serene sound track of nature, just what I needed to calm my soul. As it was the summer season in India, all the guests took to showering under the waterfall, making sure not to use chemical soaps. The locals were very protective of the mountain water and would not tolerate it being polluted and poisoned by uncaring tourists.

After hearing I had come to the Himalayas to train for a marathon, my host Ananad, advised me that a perfect challenge would be to climb Kunjapuri temple. He drew me a rough map, and early the following morning, off I set. As I was passing the waterfall, I met up with a guy named Ignio. As luck would have it, he was a semi-professional athlete in training for the Madrid marathon, and just like me, he was hill-climbing in order to strengthen his calf and thigh muscles. We decided to team up and set off together towards Kunjapuri. We had gone a third of the way when Ignio realised I was beginning to struggle. He suggested we turn back and try again the next day, and although my mind protested, my body had to agree. The following morning, at the crack of dawn, we set off again, and this time we managed to complete two-thirds of the journey. On the third morning, just as the sun was peeking over the horizon in the east, I surprised Ignio by being first to our meeting place at the waterfall. "I hear they sell the best sugarcane juice in the world at the steps of Kunjapuri Mandir," I said teasingly. He laughed excitedly, and once again, we set off on our quest. After six hours and six rest breaks, Ignio proudly bought our first round of sugarcane drinks, and I bought the second. It was the sweetest, most delicious thing we had ever tasted. After quenching our thirst, we climbed the last three hundred and twenty-nine steps to the sacred temple at the summit. From up there, at the height of 1676 metres, the panoramic views of snow-capped mountains and peaks such as Swarga Rohini and Banderpunch were spectacular. Even the birds were flying below us. As we caught our breath and took in the scenery, Ignio turned to me and confessed. "After that first day," he said. "I was convinced you wouldn't be able to climb to the top, and I was considering going it alone. After the second day, I was impressed enough to meet with you for the third attempt. And now I know that you are indeed a man of grit and determination. So, on that note…would you like to join me again tomorrow?"

We both laughed, and I told him that I had thought the same as him on that first day. But now that I had proved myself, I would be honoured to join him again. So, for the next three weeks, we climbed Kunjapuri at least fifteen more times, managing during one attempt to complete the climb in only four hours.   My thighs and calves had grown strong alongside my physical and mental well-being. Spending time in such blissful surroundings had given me a wonderful sense of inner peace. And to cap it all, the temple priest gave us his blessings to send us on our way. "Your life ahead will be like the marathon," he said. " Run it well. When you struggle the most, that is when you must increase your determination to finish. When you are in pain in the marathon and in life, use that pain as your motivation to reach the finish line. Run the marathon of life well."

On my return to London, my first job was to buy a new pair of trainers as on my final climb up Kunjapuri I had completely torn my last pair. I travelled to London Docklands to register for the marathon at the Excel exhibition centre, and while I was there, I treated myself to a new pair of trainers from the Adidas stand. I already knew it was not the best of ideas to run a marathon in a new pair of trainers. It worried me, even more, when one of the organisers suggested that I pull out of the marathon altogether as there wasn't time for me to do nearly enough training in my new footwear. It was highly likely that if I went ahead, I could cause myself permanent damage. Although I thanked him for his advice, I decided to ignore it completely.

The day of the marathon arrived, and by six in the morning, Edgware station was packed and buzzing with marathon runners and their supporters. I hadn't asked or expected Mum and Dad to come as I knew the crowds would be too much for them. But I couldn't help thinking how amazing it would have felt to have my son and daughter there cheering me on. I missed them so much, and I couldn't help imagining what they would have said to me and the look of pride on their faces as they cheered me on. But sadly, this wasn't to be, and I brushed the emotional thoughts to the back of my mind as I focussed on the enormous challenge ahead.

I made my way to my starting point in Greenwich, soaking up the carnival atmosphere and smiling to myself at some of the incredible costumes. There were runners dressed as rhinos to raise funds to save the creatures from extinction. There were others dressed as Wombles of Wimbledon Common and another group encased in a boat costume to raise money for the Royal National Lifeboat Institution. I navigated the crowds until I found my fellow St. Luke's Hospice runners, and before we knew it, we were off.

Due to the sheer volume of runners, even though the race started at 10 am, we didn't cross the starting line until 10.32 am, but right from the very beginning, I was overwhelmed by the level of support from the crowds. The cheering and clapping provided a much needed boost to my confidence, and I was happy to see so many supporters from the Sikh community handing out my favourite Indian sweets. Every time I shouted out, "Jo bole soh nihal," they would shout back, "Sat sri Akaal," and off I would run with another handful of jelebies and ladoos.

Before too long, a group of soldiers running for Help the Heroes charity overtook me, and at the nine-mile mark, feeling inordinately proud of my progress, I had to look twice as an elderly lady ran ahead of me. With my pride well and truly punctured, I picked up my pace and caught up with the woman to ask her age.

"I'm seventy-nine," she replied in a thick American accent. "Why? Do you want to ask me out?"

"I would love to, ma'am," I replied. "But I don't think I would be able to keep up with you!"

She laughed and sped ahead of me again, leaving me red-faced in her wake. But her spirit of defiance against age reminded me of one of the reasons I had decided to run the marathon in the first place. In the days when I had written for the Asian Voice Newspaper, I had been privileged to interview a guy named Mr Fauja Singh. This superhero started running at eighty-one, an age when most people have trouble even walking unaided. Incredibly, at the age of ninety-three, he ran his first marathon, The Canadian Waterfront Marathon. A year later, when he ran the Edinburgh Marathon, he officially became the oldest marathon runner in the world. Mr Singh was ninety-six when I interviewed him, and when I asked him what made him take up running at such an age, he merely smiled and replied, "I was not ready to die so young." He looked me in the eye. "What's your excuse, young man, for not stepping up a gear?"

Of course, I did not have an answer.

A week later, I interviewed another superhero, a mere baby of sixty-five, when he retired from his career as a chartered accountant. John Corner used his life savings to invest in buying a three-bedroom semi-detached house in Harrow. He converted the upstairs into office space and the downstairs into a place where the terminally ill could be looked after and cared for when the NHS could no longer help. His selfless initiative attracted so many volunteers and donations that in the year 2000, Queen Elizabeth officially opened what today is St. Luke's Hospice in Kenton. The hospice has twelve beds for the use of resident patients during the last days of their lives. The patients are provided with the most exemplary care, love, and support to ensure their final days are as meaningful and happy as possible. As St. Luke's operates as a charity, there is no cost to patients or families. Hundreds of outpatients are seen free of charge; there is a play area for terminally ill children and children whose parents are terminally sick; volunteer hairdressers are available to patients, and volunteer gardeners maintain the beautiful gardens for the patients to enjoy. It costs around £4 million a year to run St. Luke's, of which the government contributes a third. The rest of the money is raised through charitable events, such as midnight sponsored walks, volunteer-run charity shops, and of course, the London Marathon. So, even though a seventy-nine year old lady had just overtaken me, I was delighted to be finally doing my bit.

At around the twelve-mile mark, I was relieved to find that my breathing was still steady, and my calf and thigh muscles were not yet aching. But worryingly, my metatarsal bones on both feet were beginning to hurt, and although I did my best to ignore the pain, I was forced to stop at the fourteen-mile mark and made my way to the St. John's Ambulance camp for some much needed TLC. A lovely volunteer removed my trainers and socks and gave my feet a greatly appreciated massage. She told me that given the state of my feet, I would be better off giving up on the idea of completing the race and should instead take one of the sweeper buses designated to pick up any runners unable to finish.

Deep down, I knew her advice was sound, but all I could think of were the wise words of the priest at Kunjapuri, who had asked me to use my pain as a weapon to accomplish my goals in life. With his words ringing in my ears, I thanked the St. John's Ambulance volunteer for her help and advice and told her, "I am running for my life. Whatever it takes, I will cross that finishing line."

I set off with renewed determination, but by the sixteen-mile mark, the pain in my feet had become so intense that I realised my chances of actually running the final ten miles were pretty hopeless. But my resolve was far greater than the pain, and after meeting a lady named Karla, who was also on the verge of giving up, we agreed that we would finish the marathon together by walking at a steady pace. By the twenty-three mile mark, there were four of us, all hoping to cross the finishing line. I had slowed my pace to keep my three companions company, and although I was confident we would make it to the finish, my hopes of receiving a medal were diminishing fast. The marathon had to be completed in under eight hours for a participant to be eligible for a medal. Although I was confident I could do that, it would mean leaving my companions behind, which I was reluctant to do as we had formed such a close bond. I didn't want to abandon them for the sake of a medal, and yet at the same time, I was desperate for a medal, having worked so hard for it.

As I was battling my inner demons, Karla spoke up. "Go and get that medal," she said. "Go and get it for all of us. It will make me feel my run was all worthwhile."

That was all the motivation I needed. I wasn't walking the final straight just for me now, but for all of us. Just at that moment, I caught sight of my dear friends Hitesh and Nutan and their two kids. They had tracked me down using my phone location, and they were standing in the crowds cheering and clapping for all they were worth. Their sweet gesture filled the emptiness in my heart that had been there at the beginning of the day with the absence of my children. These guys were no less like family to me. With the warmth of their support, I flashed Karla a smile and sped away towards the finish. Hitesh, Nutan, and their kids kept me company for a mile, but for the final two and a quarter miles, I was on my own.

This was the most challenging and loneliest part of the whole run. I had left my friends behind, and the cheering crowds had disappeared. I was alone with my pain, my thoughts, and my purpose. By the time I reached the twenty-five mile mark, I was in excruciating pain. But my goal was so close; my medal was in reach. I thought of my children. If I didn't reach the finishing line, would I ever cross the line of getting my story to my children? If I gave up now, this close to victory, would I give up on my children having the chance to embrace and live the truth?

I thought of the priest again. "Use your pain as your motivation. Run the marathon and your life well."

His words pounded through my head in time to the beat of my heart, powering me onwards and onwards, until finally, I passed the twenty-six mile mark, and there was Buckingham Palace right in front of me and the finishing line just a hundred metres away. I was dragging my left foot behind me by now as I caught up with another runner, who was also limping. We grinned at each other, as with our arms held high in the air, we both approached the finishing arch and stepped over the line to be greeted by a jovial gentleman placing a medal around our necks.

I had done it. I couldn't quite believe it, and after the official photographs were taken, I limped into St. James Park, sat gratefully onto a bench, and let the tears run freely down my face. Against all the odds, I had completed the marathon and had a medal around my neck to prove it. But I knew that completing the London Marathon, as punishing as it had been, was nothing compared to the marathon of life I now had to prepare myself for. How was I going to do that? I knew for my children's sake, I would have to find a way, and with pain in my heart and body, I sat there contemplating the future.

But I couldn't stay there forever. As I struggled to get up from the bench, and with my limbs barely working, I was forced to call for a taxi to take me back to Edgware station, where Dad was there to pick me up.

I spent the next four days in recovery, soaking in the bathtub and massaging my metatarsal bones. My victory had come at a price after all. My foot was so badly injured, it was unlikely I would ever be able to run another marathon. As I lay in the bath, I wondered what price would have to be paid for the next marathon of life that I had to run. I knew I might not win it, but I knew I had to run it whatever the cost. And

I knew there would be resistance from those who didn't want the truth to come out, and many people would be hurt along the way. Would it be worth it? Was Arjun's victory, led by Krishna, worth the loss of entire clans from every princely state in India just because of the injustice inflicted upon six people? Had Krishna, Arjun, and the whole of Kurukshetra been right to act as they did? Or should Shakuni have won?

These questions plagued my every waking hour. Would it be better for future generations to live a lie and dwell in injustice despite the massive losses incurred? Should I just let go and allow my children and any children they might have to live that way, just to protect the name of their mother? Would their hate for me grow? Would their hurt grow even deeper once they discovered their hate for me was manufactured to cover up the actions of their mother? Would my son and daughter allow their own children to follow the same path of lies?

The pain I had suffered from competing in the London Marathon had been bad enough, but would I have the courage to suffer through the greater pain of life? I already knew my ex-wife didn't dare to face the truth. She refused to acknowledge that her suffering and that of her siblings and her father, who ended up in a mental institution, resulted from the actions of a mother who cheated on her husband and a grandfather who committed murder. Burying the reality under an avalanche of lies was easier for the family to live with than the truth. Would my children be happy to live a life of lies? Would they have the courage to live with this black stain, this stigma, this KALANK? Would their children be happy? Or their children's children? Where would it all stop?

I knew in my heart, it was *my* duty to put a stop to it all, and I determined to fight the battle in my own way. Just as Dharma and Adharma represent right and wrong and the difficulty of drawing a line between the two, people often justify their wrong deeds by placing the blame on situational or circumstantial predicaments. But it has to be remembered that right is right and wrong is wrong, circumstances notwithstanding. In the Mahabharata war, the Kauravas led by Duryodhana represented Adharma, and the Pandavas led by Yudhisthira symbolised Dharma. The epic battle at Kurukshetra is believed to have been between Dharma and Adharma, and the entire lesson of Gita is about following the path of Dharma. In other words, the basic duty of man.

It was my duty to fight back. I would not let the truth die.

THIRTEEN

"We are the makers of our own lives. There is no such thing as fate. Our lives are the result of our previous actions, our karma, and it naturally flows that, having been ourselves the makers of our karma, we must also be able to unmake it."

-   *Swami Vivekananda*

My battle for the truth to be heard and accepted was on-going. Our family traumas always lay just below the surface of our lives. But I had hoped that for once, while enjoying this special time together in India with Mum and Dad, they could have been put aside. But it was not to be, and I couldn't just stand back and let Mum perpetuate the lies.

I needed her to know how damaging her silence had been, particularly regarding my brother's violence towards Papa. I didn't relish speaking plainly to Mum, but I had made a promise to myself that I at least would certainly *not* stay silent.

"Mum," I said. "Why have you not spoken out to protect

your husband? You have the power to stop my brother from taking his anger out on his own father, a man now in his eighties."

It was true. Instead of standing by and allowing an old man to beaten by his own son, his body and his heart bruised black and blue, Mum could have stood up and put an end to it. But fearing my brother would prevent her from seeing her grandchildren, she chose instead, not only to stay silent, but also to voice support in defence of my brother's character. And because of her silence, her grandchildren have been living a life of lies, and their spiritual and karmic balances have taken a hit. They hate, and they dislike, but they don't know why they hate. And none of it is their fault. They only believe what they are told by the same people who are responsible for their spiritual development.

Sia's mother chose to nurture lust with other men over nurturing spiritual righteousness in her three young children. What a difference it would have made to the lives of those three had she controlled her addiction to sex and chosen instead to bestow inner strength and confidence upon her two daughters. Because of the choices she made, her daughters innocently walked along the same pathway following their 'hero.' If she had made the right choices in life, her daughters would not have imitated her lifestyle of continually searching for love from one man to another even after committing themselves in marriage. If she had made the right choices, her daughters would have inherited inner strength and the ability to find love within themselves. Sia was blessed with many unique and exceptional qualities that I rarely saw in most women I knew of her age. But having the same weakness as her mum, she too had led her children to live lives full of lies and hate. They would have to work harder in this life and even in their future lives to repay their increased karmic debts of hate. And they would have to face their children's hatred in another life or later on in this one. All because Sia viewed her mother as righteous in living a karmically damaging life.

"And you, Mum," I said. "If you had not given the reins of my life to my brother at such a young age, I believe he would not have turned into such a controlling bully. At the age of four, I would not have had to lick all that he had trodden on from the soles of his shoes in the belief that God would be happy with me for obeying him. I would have been able to choose the subjects I wanted to study for my A-levels and been happy as a history teacher rather than living through nine years of hell, unable to enjoy or understand what I was taught. You allowed his bullying nature to destroy my self-confidence. You planted the seeds that led to your own husband living in fear after becoming a punching bag for his son. Papa does not say anything. But he is scared. He lives in fear of his own flesh and blood. Have you not heard him crying while he is praying? He is terrified of the one person who was supposed to look after him in his old age. He is scared of the son he has spent his whole life providing for. The son, who he provided more than enough to have a huge three-story house to live in. The son whose children left university debt-free because of Papa. My brother destroyed my confidence when I was only a boy, Mum. And you let him. He is not all bad. Not by any means. He has many, many good qualities, including a very generous heart. This would have shone in his life. His spirituality would have shone. But now, because you did not nurture him into righteousness, his karma will have his son being violent in a future life and his grandchildren hating him after taking all his wealth."

It was so hard speaking to Mum like this. But once I'd started, I couldn't stop. She needed to face reality. "I really need you to know what is in my heart, Mother. I want you to know how I am feeling. I want you to listen and realise. I don't want you to regret missing this one opportunity to understand your own son. Please, let me express my heart to you, Mother."

She turned and began to walk away.

"Please, don't leave," I begged her. "Please, hear me out. Please."

Mum stopped in her tracks and looked around at me. There were tears in her eyes. "Tell me what is in your heart, Mayur. What has been hurting you?"

Tears then sprang to my eyes as I continued to open my heart to her. "It's not too late," I said. "You could still stop the violence. Yes, your grandchildren might shun you, but at least you would be living a righteous life. And in doing so, you can prevent your grandchildren from damaging their own karmic balance and spirituality and destroying themselves in lies and hate. But to do this, you need strength which you do not have. You need to put into practice all that you have learned from your spiritual teacher. You need to act upon all the advice and sermons you to give to my friends. Please, Mum," I begged her. "Do the right thing. Save your grandchildren's spiritual future. Save your husband. Stop your grandchildren and yourself from living incorrect lives by putting righteousness before your attachment to them."

Papa had stood by, allowing me to get my frustrations off my chest. But now, it was his turn to interrupt. He defended my brother in his usual calm manner, telling me that karma didn't always work in the way I imagined. "Your brother may have to face karma because of his bullying, but maybe you are already repaying your karma for being a bully in a previous life. And maybe my grandchildren will face hatred by their own wrongly guided grandchildren in a future life. Or, maybe, you and I are paying off our karmic debts, and they are innocently helping us. Everyone has to face their karma. No one can escape it. But it is wrong for hate to be based on lies. Those who hide the truth at all costs are the ones destroying innocence."

On that note, we decided enough was enough for one night. I didn't want to press my point so close to bedtime. And it was never a good idea to go to sleep on an argument. We hugged each other and changed the subject, discussing our plans for the following day instead. The family hug felt good, but also strange as it was a rare occurrence back in London.

The morning dawned on another glorious day. I decided to give the ladies a break from hosting and cooking and arranged a day at the beach. Despite my cousin's protestations, I insisted and booked a driver to pick the whole family up and take us the hour's drive east of Kodinar to the coastal town of Diu. This beautiful place sits at the eastern end of Diu Island and connects by bridge to the state of Gujarat. Once a Portuguese colony for over four hundred years, Diu is still steeped in the history and architecture of its European colonizers. There are crumbling Portuguese villas scattered here and there, beautiful churches, and a sixteenth century Portuguese citadel with a lighthouse and canons that sits up high overlooking the Arabian Sea. The streets of Diu are clean and quiet; the whole place so bright and fresh, it feels a million miles away from India. You could be forgiven for thinking you had landed in a different country entirely.

We settled ourselves on the beach, near a patch of shade cast by the spreading branches of a clump of Hokka trees. These unusual palm trees are native to North Africa and are unique to Diu, being found nowhere else in India. They are also known as Doum Palms or Gingerbread trees and look similar to a coconut tree, but with branches that grow out in different directions and small, red edible fruits prized for their medicinal qualities. The Duom Palm was considered sacred by ancient Egyptians, and its seeds have been found in the tombs of many pharaohs. We were just grateful for the shade these beautiful trees offered, knowing that the day ahead was going to be hot.

I looked around at my family and felt my chest swell with pride. I listened to the laughter and the chat and watched the joy flit across Mum and Dad's faces. It was wonderful to see how happy and content they were to be spending the day in such a stunning location surrounded by their loving family. We were here to enjoy ourselves and indulge in the delights of all the tasty food and beverages on offer. We certainly couldn't spend the day on the beach without sampling some of the abundance of fresh coconuts piled up in vibrant green towers on various stalls dotted around the beach. It was an event in itself to watch the coconut vendors select the perfect coconut for every individual customer. The vendors were skilled in the art of tapping the coconut shells to ascertain the thickness of the meat or jelly inside. Some customers preferred hard jelly, while others would rather have soft jelly. The vendor satisfied everyone's requests to perfection before he lopped off the top of each coconut with one swift swipe of his machete so we could enjoy the silky, refreshing milk. He even fashioned a spoon for those of us who wanted to scoop out the deliciously sweet and tender coconut flesh. Before the day was over, our little party managed to fill two large bins with empty coconut shells. I didn't bother counting how many coconuts we had devoured between us, as I was pretty sure the vendor would over-estimate and rip me off. But I wasn't overly worried as the day was drifting by so pleasantly it didn't seem worth an argument. Uncle Jitendra had other ideas, though. He had meticulously counted every coconut and, in the process, saved me from being over-charged the equivalent of a whole £3.50!

There was a vast array of other tasty treats on offer, including barbecued sweetcorn, aloo paratha, chana jor garam, and maggi noodles. It might not have been the healthiest food in the world, but it was certainly the most appetizing. From time to time, one or more of us would pad across the hot sand to dip our feet in the bracing but calm waters of the Arabian Sea. It was such a perfect day. Voices layered on top of voices, family stories retold, memories relived, jokes and laughter, and a deep sense of belonging characterised the whole day.

Midway through the afternoon, I felt the need to stretch my legs, take a walk along the beach, and perhaps help digest all the naughty but nice junk food in my belly. Mum asked if she could join me, and of course, I was only too happy to have her keep me company. We wandered away from the rest of the group down to the shoreline, where gentle waves licked the sand and cooled our hot feet. We strolled along, remarking on this and that, taking pleasure in each other's company and the sheer beauty of the scenery around us. When Mum began to tire, we found a bench looking out to sea and sat down to rest before walking back to join the rest of our group.

I had hoped that our disagreement the evening before would not be mentioned again. I didn't want anything to spoil the day, or indeed the trip. But our argument had obviously been playing on Mum's mind, so the conversation became heated once again.

"You are always taking your Dad's side," she scolded. "You two gang up against me all the time. Your brother supports me, though. He took me to America. He is a good man." She lifted her chin in defiance.

"Oh, Mother," I said, exasperated. "If he is such a good man, why would he use his eighty-two-year-old father as a punching bag? He lives in a huge house, thanks to Dad, and his children are free from university debts because Dad gave them tens of thousands of pounds. What has my father not done for this so-called 'good man?' Did my brother invite Dad to America too? No. In fact, you only told Papa the night before you were flying. And you say you are a good wife?"

"That wasn't my fault," grumbled Mum. "I was told not to mention anything."

"But, it is your fault, Mother," I insisted. "It is your fault that Papa is enduring violence, and you have kept quiet about it because the person inflicting the violence is your son. It is your fault that you have always placed more importance on people liking you rather than on what is right or wrong."

I knew there were many reasons behind my brother's violence towards Dad. But there were no excuses. There was nothing in the world that could justify a son lashing out at his elderly father, punching him, and tossing him a dustbin. Yes, my brother harboured jealousies. He hated that I was taller than him. He hated that I had made friends easily at school when nobody wanted to play with him, nobody except me – and he hated that Dad still stood by me even when my own children took against me in the aftermath of my acrimonious divorce. He hated that I had come to live in Mum and Dad's house and that Dad had refused to kick me out even when his own grandchildren threatened not to see him again if he didn't. But none of that gave him the right to physically hurt our father.

"It isn't my fault," Mum repeated. "My spiritual teacher said I would not improve until many lifetimes."

"Then why is Papa already a better person now?" I challenged her. "You both have the same teacher. For years I would curse and swear at your teacher for taking your inner self away from us. But then I realised, it was not the teacher. It was you, getting carried away preaching, putting your own angle on everything you learned."

"You are wrong," said Mum. "I was told to take the message of God door to door. And I was told I would not improve in this lifetime. Also, your Dad is not a good man, and you hate me."

"Oh, Mummy. Of course, I don't hate you," I said. "But I have very little respect for you. The devotion of a son to his mother, his first God, is no longer there. You remind me of my ex-wife's late mother. Both of you put your mind's desires before the spiritual well-being of your children. As long as you receive your short-term hits, it matters not if it destroys your children."

Mum shook her head. "No. Your ex-wife told me that her poor mother was murdered by her drunken father-in-law after being raped by him every day, even when she was on her monthly cycle. And the day she refused to have sex with him was the day he stabbed her."

"Yes," I said. "That is what Sia led me to believe, too, when I first met her. That is what she told everybody. And I hated her grandfather, thinking he was a rapist, an alcoholic, and a murderer. Yes, it was an unforgivable and evil thing that he did, but he was not an alcoholic or a rapist. He was angry. Angry at his daughter-in-law for cheating on his son. Angry that she had no shame in publically and openly having multiple affairs. Angry at her for putting her pleasure in other men before the well-being of his grandchildren. She even had affairs with two men at the same time. Not that this excuses his 'honour killing' in any way. It was a despicable act. He took away the mother of three lovely children. That can never be forgiven. But what Sia's mother did was selfish, and she cannot have truly loved her children. If she had only fallen in love with one man, that would have been somewhat understandable, as she had been forced into marriage. But before the affairs with the two men, there had been another. She had been warned not to see him anymore as he was a relative, and she even called him brother."

"Don't give me a big lecture and don't compare me to that woman," said Mum. "I did not sleep around."

"No, Mummy," I said. "You have higher standards than that lady."

Mum looked at me. "When Sia left taking your children, it must have been painful. Is it still painful?"

"Her leaving? No," I said. "She was never mine, going from one man to another from day one. I was attached to her because I was weak. Her taking the children has broken my heart over and over again every single day. But what can I do? If the children have chosen to hate me because of the lies they were fed and have been brought up with, lies that were injected in them over and over again, I can only, once in a while, cry and pray that the truth reaches them. And when it does, I don't want them to hate their mum. I just want them to stop hating me. And I want them to stop punishing their own karmic balance, which is sure to balance itself out in future lives. And if they do come back to me, all will be forgiven towards their mother for such a selfish life of putting lust before her children living lives of righteousness."

"Have you let go of your wife's affairs?" asked Mum.

"Ex-wife," I corrected her. "Yes, I have. To me, there are two Sias, Mum. The Sia I first met; the innocent, loving, romantic young lady I started dating in 1988. The one I wanted to love and be loved by and dreamed of having a happy family life with. And then there's the other Sia, the woman she became, always running from one man to another as if it was an addiction and then desperately wanting to hide the truth from the world and abusing her children by leading them into lives of hate and lies. The first Sia I shall always treasure in a special place in my heart. I will forever be grateful for the special memories and our two wonderful children. But the second Sia, my dignity and self-integrity will not allow me to look at or think about. I was so hurt every time I caught her out in her affairs. And every time she told me the same thing – "it was my one mistake." But I caught her out so many times, it led to me becoming completely paranoid and suspecting her of sleeping with everyone. But the DNA results were the worst hurt of all. She may as well have stuck a knife in my heart. Weeks before marrying me, she was sleeping with another man. And if the baby wasn't his, then her behaviour was even worse than I could have imagined."

I sighed. "Finding out the truth was my downfall, and I was punished for that. My son and daughter hate me. When I went to see my son at university, he walked away without even looking at me. Then, when I read what he had written about me during the harassment court case, I realised why my children hate me. They had been led to believe that it was me, and not their mother, who had slept around, that it was me, and not their mother, who had cheated. All of your three grandsons believed these lies, Mummy. And why wouldn't they? It was their living gods who told them. Why wouldn't they believe their living gods? And now, not knowing the truth, they will be happy to hate me for the rest of their lives. They will not even want to know the truth; despite all the evidence, they will not have the courage to accept it. They will be happy to live a lie forever."

"But, they told me your evidence was fabricated," said Mum.

"How can DNA results be fabricated?"

"They said you did not use your daughter's hair sample alongside your own."

I sighed again in exasperation. "Mummy, Mummy, Mummy. Listen to me. Nobody would believe me. They told me I was lying. Yet, they kept refusing to take part in a DNA test. They refused in 2006, twice in 2007, and again in 2008. If they truly believed I was lying, why would they refuse the one thing that would prove their allegation? Just before the court case, my daughter agreed to the test, just to shut me up, she said. Then a few days later, she changed her mind again. If they were so adamant I was wrong, why not take the test to prove it? But I wasn't wrong, was I? I even have a letter from my ex-wife's lover confessing to his affairs with her: one just before our Indian marriage and another towards the end of our marriage. As I said, Mummy, truth is stranger than fiction. A harsh truth may not be believed for a long, long time. It will be covered up by a mountain of lies that will eventually collapse like an avalanche. And because I have evidence to support that truth, the attempts to cover it increased dramatically. All my friends and relatives were fed lies, but only those with courage stood by the truth. The mentally weak did not want to get involved. They did not want to challenge what they wanted to believe. Yet, the weak will always shout the loudest against perceived injustice."

"I know you have been through a lot," said Mum. "But

why are you comparing me to that woman who slept around?"

"I am not comparing you to her," I replied. "Your standards are vastly higher than hers. But just like she was addicted to men, you are addicted to attention and compliments. You crave the good opinion of others, especially your grandchildren's. You want them to like you and say nice things about you. And just like Sia's mother put her addiction before her children, you put your addiction before your children."

I paused for a moment and looked out at the calm surface of the sea glittering under the sun. I wished I felt as tranquil, but I didn't. Waves of emotion were crashing around inside me, and although I wouldn't have chosen to have this conversation with Mum at this time and in this place, it had started now. There was no going back. The turmoil I had suffered for the last few years had to be spoken about, and Mum had to know the part that she had played in that. I turned back to her. "Mummy," I said. "You are the one person who could have put an end to all the lies. You could have stopped an old man from being beaten up. You could have challenged my brother and my daughter over the DNA test. But you chose to keep quiet. My brother has been a bully all his life, and his bullying only increased after his marriage. Do you know why some people love to bully and control others?"

Mum didn't answer, so I stood up to make my point. "Because it makes them feel good to have control over people weaker than themselves. And yet they are scared of people they deem more powerful than themselves." I looked at Mum pointedly. "Only people without minds of their own would follow a bully."

I sat down on the bench again. "My brother was happy to take all the money Dad gave him, yet he repaid this generosity with violence. You could have stopped it all, but you kept quiet just because Dad had an affair thirty-five years ago."

"No," said Mum. "It was not because of the affair. Because Papa took your side, our grandchildren refused to see him. That's why he was not invited to America."

I looked at her askance. "So you allowed my brother to blackmail you? To do as he said, or he would cut you off from your grandchildren? Shame on you, Mother. Shame on you. And you claim to uphold such a high and mighty religious stance." I took a deep breath. "Is being told you are wonderful, worth turning a blind eye to violent injustice suffered by an old man? Have you no other purpose but to hear those words? All the knowledge and spiritual strength you gained from your spiritual teacher was solely to hear the words, 'you are wonderful'?"

Mum's eyes flashed. " 'I worked very hard for that knowledge. I excelled at every spiritual examination. I got higher marks than your father. It showed my competence. It gave me pride. Why should I not be proud of this? Why should I not hear that people are proud of me? Should I not hear 'Well done. You're wonderful?'"

"Think about it, Mother. This knowledge that you have so proudly gained, how have you actually implemented it to turn it into wisdom?"

"I distributed it to others. I went to people's houses to tell them about our teacher and his great teachings so that they can implement it in their lives, too."

"Not everyone is a great teacher like your spiritual teacher Pandurang Shastri, Mum, or a great distributor of righteousness like Mahatma Gandhi. With all this wonderful knowledge of yours, you could have imparted some wisdom to your son to show him how to act correctly towards his father. By taking a stance, you could have stopped his violence. Ever since I was a child, you allowed him to be a bully. You even encouraged him. You allowed him to bully me and then his own father. You could have shown him the path of love, humility, and compassion. You could have shown him all that your teacher has shown you. My brother has leadership skills. He could have been a great leader. Both Mahatma Gandhi and Adolf Hitler were leaders with great influence," I said sarcastically. "I love my brother," I continued. "You may not believe this, but I really do love him. I know he has many wonderful qualities, despite his controlling, bullying ways. But his violence towards Papa is unforgivable. You could have stopped this, Mum. Instead, you inflamed this side of his nature by keeping quiet, even as your own husband was being hurt. You have it in your power to stop all this," I went on. "By staying silent and not speaking out, you are allowing an old man to be hurt over and over again, and you are allowing your grandchildren to live a lie."

I knew Mum was scared that if she spoke out, her grandchildren would shun her the same as they shunned Dad and me. I think she was frightened that because Dad was seven years older than her and likely to die first, she would be the one left to take any blame. I tried to make her see this was not a good enough reason to stay silent. "Because of your silence, Mum, so many people are suffering. Because you are addicted to attention and praise, and you put these needs of yours above everything else, the truth is being buried. You must recognise that, surely?"

I remembered how Dad had stood by his Gita teachings and followed the path of righteousness when my brother tried to turn him against me. "I'm not going to tell Mayur to leave my house," Dad had said. "I am not going to shun him. He is my son. And if my refusing to kick him out means that I lose the lot of you, then so be it. It will hurt me a lot, and I will cry many tears, but I will not do an injustice to my son."

A cool breeze ruffled the fabric of Mum's Punjabi dress

as she looked down at the ground. "All I wanted is for you and your brother to be happy," she said. "I am a mother. I have nothing but boundless love for you both."

"But Mummy," I said. "Love is supposed to guide children towards success and teach them right from wrong and the difference between appropriate and inappropriate actions. If it had been love you were showering down, then you would not have turned your cheek on a great evil, nor would my brother be trapped in a life of unrighteousness. If you have the courage to acknowledge the truth, then you will know that what you gave was not love but attachment to needing to be liked. And according to the Bhagwad Gita classes I attend, love and attachment are opposites."

Mum frowned. "But attachment comes from love. It is because of my love for you and your brother and my four grandchildren that I am attached to you all."

"No, Mummy. No. Where there is true love, there is no attachment. Love is born out of compassion. Attachment is born from arrogance. Didn't we learn that from Bhagwad Gita? I still have a lot of love for my brother. That is why I pray that God gives him every happiness. But because of his violence, I cannot give him the happiness of my respect. Love would not make you proud of what he has become. Only attachment can make you proud of a violent thug, like Dhidhastra's blind attachment for unrighteous Duryodhan. Attachment to my brother and his children has made you turn a blind eye. Love would liberate your children and grandchildren. Attachment binds them. Because where there is love, there is no attachment."

"But why would I not want to bind with my children and grandchildren?" Mum asked.

I summoned up some more patience. "The actions that led to the murder of Sia's mother were all born out of attachments. Sia's mother was attached to sex and, therefore, men. Her father-in-law was attached to his son, who she constantly cheated on. Her husband was attached to her and had a mental breakdown after her death, ending up in an asylum. Her daughters were attached to her and followed in her behavioural footsteps. Her granddaughter, my daughter, was attached to her mum and started hating me even though I was being cheated on. And Sia's attachment to our son made her lie to him about me. Attachment has caused this family to break apart. Both Sia and her mother were firmly attached to physical relationships. Had they tried to control this urge and their disenchantment with their husbands, or at least divorced their husbands rather than having affairs, they would have taught their children about love, not lust, fear, and hatred. Because of these addictive attachments, in truth, they were never really true mothers. They were nothing but bad teachers. Not only did they poison their own minds but also the minds of their children. They destroyed their children's innocence. Can you not see that, Mummy? All this damage because of attachment."

"But what about your father's attachment to you?" Mum challenged.

"It is not attachment. It is love," I explained. "Papa had the wisdom to put into practice all the knowledge he gained from your Gita classes. You both had the choice of whether to give in to my brother's blackmail or not. He told you he and your four grandchildren would shun you if you did not take away my inheritance. You were weak. You have chosen not to give a penny to me in your will, so you can still have your attachment to all of them, knowing full well I would not shun you no matter what. Papa also knew that I would be with him no matter what. Yet, despite knowing I would never abandon him, he kept his righteousness before his attachment. He did not stop loving anyone. If someone loves you for your wealth, have they ever loved you? Papa's heart is broken, not his love for anyone. He has something you don't have, Mother, and that is the courage to practice the Bhagwad Gita. Because of Papa, I will be giving my half of the inheritance to the children of the very same man who wants to take it away from me. My brother."

Mum raised her eyebrows. "I am happy that you will do that. But I don't believe you. Why would you give your inheritance to your brother's children?"

"Simple," I said. "Because I love them. Your four grandchildren are my four candles. And if I can't be their friend, at least if they learn the truth, maybe I can stop being their enemy."

"Four Candles? That's the name of your lifestyle coaching company?"

"Yes. I named my company Four Candles because they are my four candles. And the more pain their hate gives me, the more I will love them from my heart. The more I will pray for their souls. It does not matter if they do not wish me happiness; there will always be a wish and prayer for their happiness in my heart. All I wanted, Mummy, was a happy family life. All of us together and in one house. It was my dream. A happy, united family. But my dream was broken when someone woke me up to the dark reality. Maybe because of my karma in a previous life, I was destined to feel this pain. But it pains me more that my four candles are now destined for this unbearable pain in future lives. Their own living Gods have increased the karmic debts for themselves and their children and future generations. Why mother? Why is life so unfair? Why can't I have what I want? Why has my discovery of two truths broken all ties with my four candles? Why did I not just turn a blind eye to these truths for the sake of my four angels? First, I lost my children when I discovered my ex-wife's affairs and took the DNA test. And then I lost my brother's two children when I discovered his violence towards Papa. Why is it that the guilty are not punished? Why is the innocent one going through this pain?

Why is life so unfair mother?" I leant my head on her shoulder and cried for the first time.

She gently stroked my hair. "You have gone through a lot of tears. What can I do to wipe them?" Mummy asked her little (big) boy.

"Just don't give me a reason to cry again," I pleaded. "Tell my brother that you will take a stance if Papa is beaten again. And if you are daring, tell my son the truth, please. Even if their living Gods turn them away from you."

"We are all to blame," said Mum. "Including you, my son. Your ex-wife hid the truth from your children, but did you show them love? You reacted with anger towards all of us. Towards me for revealing the cracks in our family to the outside world. That was my fault. Your daughter's fault was that despite knowing the truth about the DNA results, she decided to hide it from her brother. Maybe to protect her mother or maybe to protect him from further pain. You need to control your anger no matter what wrong people do to you. Even towards me, you are angry. You have never forgiven me for interfering in your family. My intentions were only to help, out of love. I can understand this was wrong now. But let go of this anger towards me now. I will tell your brother to control his anger towards your dad."

I put my arms around her. "I love you a lot Mummy, I said. "More than you believe."

"If your love is so strong, then anger is an unusual way

of showing it," she said. "I am your mother."

She was right. I did not like myself at that moment. Yes, she had been wrong for interfering and also for turning a blind eye. But my anger must have caused her a lot of pain.

Mum and I sat in silence for a moment, deep in thought. It was Mum who spoke again first. "Why do you say I am weak and I do not put Gita into practice? You know I get better results than your father in every class test. For forty-one years, I went every week to those classes and participated in all of their programs. Then I went door to door to the houses of Gujarati people and recited to them the lessons I had learned. I have put into practice the things I learned far more so than your Papa. I have lived a true disciple's life."

I shook my head. "Mother, you might be more knowledgeable than Papa, but have you not noticed how he has changed in his later years? How he has dedicated himself to living his life differently? How he has truly focussed on being the best student and putting into practice everything he has learned? Your focus has been on imparting your knowledge to other people instead of implementing it into your own life. A true disciple is one who lives like Arjun of Mahabharat. A true disciple is one for whom the Almighty Lord forgets His hierarchy to come and sit at His disciple's feet and take control of his own life's chariot. That is the reason I chose the name Arjun for my son. So that Krishna can guide his chariot of life, and so that he has the courage to stand up for truth and righteousness no matter what."

"What is it you want from me?" asked Mum, raising her voice in agitation. "Do you want me to give you the whole house? Do you want me to sever my relationships with five people to keep a relationship with only one?"

"What I want or don't want is not important," I replied. "I don't want your half of the house. I will eventually give Dad's half to my brother's children. And I will certainly not be happy if you sever your relationship with them. It would actually break my heart to know that your heart was broken. But you can grant me one wish. And that is, please treat my brother and me equally. For once in your life, do the right thing. And do it without fear."

"But I do treat you equally."

"Mummy, we both know that's a lie."

Her eyes glinted with indignation. "Tell me," she said. "Have I not lived a righteous life? In what way did I live an unrighteous life? Have I not sacrificed myself for my family? What fault of mine are you so upset about?'

"Ignorance is your sin, Mother. You have never tried to know the true wisdom of righteousness or the true value of compassion towards your husband. You only ever think about yourself and what people think and say about you. You are so concerned about the opinions of your eldest son and four grandchildren that you have never allowed yourself to condemn the violence my brother wrought on Papa. You never put into practice the righteousness you were taught. And the word selfishness hides behind your meaning of sacrifice."

"But ever since marriage, I have sacrificed myself," Mum argued. "To the needs and wants of my husband, my mother-in-law, my children, and my grandchildren. I religiously served my family. I was never disloyal to the family. In all of this, there was no selfishness."

"Yes, Mother. Your loyalty and dedication are surely great deeds. You have certainly put a lot of effort and energy into your family. But when you talk of sacrifice, what drove you to sacrifice your responsibility towards righteousness?"

Mum hesitated before answering. "I kept silent to avoid internal conflicts within the family, to avoid the rift within the family from getting any bigger, and to protect the family from the harm that would come of people knowing. It was my duty to stay silent."

"But can you not see," I tried to tell her gently. "Everything that you tried to protect by your silence has been destroyed by your silence. Your silence has made the rifts, and the conflicts grow ever bigger. Think about it, Mummy. Your silence has caused the opposite to happen of everything you wanted your silence to achieve. My understanding of duty, as taught by the Bhagwad Gita, is to make a decision. The correct decision and then to accept the outcome of that decision. But when did you make a righteous decision, Mummy? When your husband was getting punched, what decision did you take? To remain silent. You made the decision not to be shunned by your grandchildren and your eldest son, knowing that I would be angry at you but that I would never shun you. In reality, you ran away from your responsibility to make rightful decisions on the pretext of doing your duty by keeping silent. Think about it, Mother. What have you done that is so great for my brother? Did you give him the wisdom of righteousness when he was pummelling his fists into an old man? Did you teach him to take the pathway of non-violence? Did you give him any wisdom to negate his greed for his father's wealth?'

"But your brother is giving this wealth to your children as well," said Mum.

"Yes, I know he is," I replied. "But that is only because he doesn't want the money to go to my children through me. He doesn't want my son to start thinking good of me in case he gets close to the truth. Please, Mummy, if you want to do one thing right by me, please help me get the truth back to my son. And I will give you all the evidence you need to substantiate my truth."

Mum glared at me. "No," she said. "If I do that, they will shun me just like they shun your father, and the two of you will only argue with me every day after that." She pushed out her bottom lip and folded her arms over her chest. "I was having a great holiday with you. But now you have ruined it by telling me everything is all my fault. I never want to come to India with you again."

I wished with all my heart that there had never been a need for this conversation, but I had promised to uphold the truth, and I hoped that one day Mum would come to understand that.

Luckily, our argument did not spoil the rest of the day, and when we returned to the family group, the laughter and good times continued and were captured in precious photographs, which I treasure to this day.

Later, as I contemplated what had transpired between Mum and me on the beach, I thought about how Dad had reacted to my brother's violence with such dignity and lack of reproach. "He has forgotten I am his father," he had said. "He has forgotten who I am. But I have not forgotten who he is. The day he was born was the proudest day of my life. He took his first steps holding on to my thumb, and when we lived in Africa, where apples were so expensive, I always brought one home for him because it was his favourite fruit. I had such high hopes for him. I thought he would make you the best big brother, which is why I allowed him to choose what subjects you should study at school. Yes, he may have forgotten who I am. But I will never forget he is my firstborn son."

Dad was truly a living God, with a soul so full of

forgiveness, light, and generosity of spirit. I couldn't have admired or loved him any more.

FOURTEEN

"Devotion is the realisation that wealth, education and power are God given gifts and not the endowments of fate."

-   *Pandurang Shastri Athavale*

With our excursion to the beach safely stored away in our memory banks as a day to treasure and with the last grains of sand brushed from our feet, Mum and Dad prepared themselves to meet up with members of their religious organisation for a much anticipated trip.

The Swadhyaya Movement (or Swadhyaya Parivar) was a religious movement extremely close to Mum and Dad's hearts and one they had belonged to for several decades. Swadhyay is a Sanskrit word meaning the study, knowledge, and discovery of the 'Self,' and Parivar, meaning family. It is a relatively new movement founded in the mid-1900s in the western states of India and our home state of Gujarat by an Indian activist and spiritual leader named Pandurang Shastri Athavale (fondly known as Dada, meaning elder brother). During one of his devotional visits to Mumbai, Dada encouraged a small group of co-workers to participate in similar visits to several villages in Bombay to spread the concept of an indwelling God to cultivate increased self-respect, respect for others, and abandonment of immoral behaviour. The villages where Swadhyay flourished experienced a reduction in crime, the removal of social barriers, and a radical decrease in poverty, homelessness, and other undesirable social conditions.

Swadhyay is a quiet movement concerned with the religion of a human being rather than aligning to traditional organised religions such as Christianity, Buddhism, Judaism, or Hinduism. It shuns publicity, does not belong to any religious body, has no form of dogma, and does not accept financial help for any of its projects or gatherings. It has achieved remarkable results in helping to create a society filled with devotion and self-discipline which values attitude over action, thoughts over things, group over the individual, and truth over logic.

Mum and Dad were true devotees, and as I waved them off, I could see how excited and grateful they were to be heading off to meet their dear friends and fellow devotees. It would certainly be a quiet few days without them. Still, I was confident they would make up for that on their return by regaling me non-stop with tales of their adventures - I decided I had better make the most of the temporary peace.

I set off to meet my new girlfriend Suji to spend some time together in Mumbai.

Mum and Dad's first stop off was the beautiful coastal city of Porbandar, lying sedately in the Saurashtra Peninsula, and best known for being the birthplace of Mahatma Gandhi.

Born Mohandas Karamchand Gandhi on October 2, 1869, Gandhi was the youngest child of his father's fourth wife. His father was chief minister of Porbander and his mother, Putlibai, was a deeply religious woman. She wasn't one for chasing riches or possessions. She led a simple life of devotion, worshipping the Hindu God Vishnu and following the teachings of Jainism and the belief that everything in the universe is eternal. Gandhi grew up taking 'ahimsa' for granted (the ancient Indian principle of non-violence, which applies to all living beings) as well as veganism, fasting, and mutual tolerance between all religious creeds and sects.

Gandhi wasn't a gifted scholar. The educational facilities in Porbandar were pretty basic, with students using their fingers to write the alphabet in the dust on the ground. Yet, he grew up to become a lawyer, politician, social activist, writer, and leader of the nationalist movement against the British rule of India. In the eyes of millions of his fellow Indians, he came to be revered as the Mahatma (Great Soul), the father of his country and internationally esteemed for his policy of non-violent protest to achieve social and political advancement. Mahatma Gandhi's name is now one of the most universally recognised on our planet, and his image graces every Indian banknote.

Mum and Dad greatly enjoyed the beauty of Porbandar, with its impressive stone buildings with ashlar masonry, carved windows, and gateways, and the ancient jetties at the port, which served as a reminder of the days when the city was a hub for maritime activities. They marvelled at the many temples scattered around Porbandar, the piercing blueness of the sea, and, of course, had the chance to visit Kirti Mandir, the memorial house kept in memory of Gandhi. Converted into a small museum, Kirti Mandir lies adjacent to Gandhi's ancestral home and houses a library of books written by Gandhi or pertaining to his philosophies. The house of his birth can be accessed from inside the museum and is filled with paintings of Gandhi and rare black and white photographs of him and his wife, Kasturba. It is a place where many world leaders come to pay their respects and a place where there is something intangible in the air, something peaceful and calming.

FIFTEEN

"Swadhyay is to study and read all the subtle differences of the mind be still and observe."

- *Dr. Shardha Batra*

On the morning of February 19, 2019, Mum and Dad along with their friends from Swadhyay - Keshavjibhai and his wife Ramaben, and Shamjibhai (bhai meaning brother and ben meaning sister in our culture) set off for the tortoise-shaped 'not quite an island' of Kutch. They were all travelling together in an enormous SUV, but when Mum appeared with her equally enormous suitcase, it soon became clear separate travel arrangements would have to be made for her luggage as there was no way it would fit in the vehicle.

Mum didn't like wearing traditional Punjabi dresses – simple cotton tops and trousers – that she could fold up into small packages and hence into a small suitcase. No. Mum preferred to wear saris with their voluminous layers of fabric and accompanying petticoats and blouses. And, of course, Mum needed a clean set every day. Because she was worried about not being able to find a reliable dhobi on her travels who could wash her clothes (even though these days dhobi's have state of the art washing machines to replace the traditional method of rivers and rocks), she had to ensure she had enough outfits to last the duration of the trip. So, her suitcase travelled to Kutch in solitary splendour and was reunited with Mum when they reached 'The White Desert of India,' as Kutch is also known.

Kutch was once a princely state of India and still manages to hold on to its past grandeur. With its vast expanses of white, salt desert, it is probably one of the country's most beautiful yet surreal places. Lying on the Indian-Pakistan border, it's also famous for its embroidery and crafts, flamingo sanctuary, and long stretches of stunning beaches. But it had been a long journey, and everyone was tired. The exploring would have to wait until the following day. In the meantime, Shamjibbhai was dropped off at his house in Surajpur, and Keshavjibhai and Ramaben were dropped at their house in Mirjapur. Mum fell totally in love with Keshavjibhai and Ramaben's house, telling them it was even more splendid than their London house. Everyone bid each other a good night as they planned for an early start in the morning.

By 7 o'clock the next day, everyone was up and ready

and eager to go. Their first port of call was Mandvi beach, a sprawling stretch of soft golden sand on the southern tip of Gujarat, lying alongside its namesake of a town that was once a thriving port. The beach itself is charming. It is pristine, serene, and calm, with a backdrop of gently whirring windmills. As well as the smooth sands and vivid blue sea, there are camel rides to be enjoyed, balloon rides, ATV's and bustling snack stalls selling the traditional offerings of fresh coconuts, barbecued sweetcorn basted in salt, lemon, and red chilli powder and a whole host of other lip-smacking Gujarati dishes.

After a morning spent in these beautiful, serene surroundings watching locals and tourists enjoying the activities on offer, and sampling some of the delicious sweetcorn, washed down with fresh coconut water, of course, it was time for Mum and Dad and their friends to set off to their next planned destination.

They loved to visit temples, and the Swaminarayan Mandir in Mandvi was a stunning example of one of over a thousand Swaminarayan temples spread across five continents. Mum and Dad were already familiar with the Swaminarayan Mandir in Neasdon, London, being one of the most opulent and the first authentic Hindu temple built in Europe. Designed and constructed according to ancient Vedic architectural texts, it was built using entirely traditional methods, avoiding the use of modern materials such as steel and iron. It cost £12 million and required almost 3,000 tonnes of Bulgarian limestone and 2,000 tonnes of Italian marble. A team of 1,500 sculptors in Gujarat carved and prepared more than 26,000 individually numbered chunks of stone which were then shipped back to London to be assembled as part of the main mandir building.

HH Shrajree Ghanshyam Maharaj, the founder of the Swaminarayan Sampraday, established and constructed the first nine Swaninarayan temples in the cities of Ahmedabad, Bhuj, Muli, Vadtal, Junagadh, Dholera, Dholka, Gadhpur, and Jetalpur as part of his philosophy of theism and deity worship. The temples are all built using traditional temple architecture to reflect the importance of Krishna and all house shrines and reverential idols. Like other Hindu temples, Swaminarayan temples feature walkways allowing worshippers to keep their right shoulders towards the shrine as they walk around it. The main shrine area is divided by railings with one side reserved for women as Swaninarayan believes that men and women should be separated in temples to fully concentrate on God.

A devastating earthquake in 2001 destroyed much of the nearby city of Bhuj, including the original Shri Swam-inarayan Mandir, built in 1824. A new temple was duly constructed using only marble and gold at the cost of one billion Indian rupees. Swaminarayan's throne, the temple domes, and doors are all gold, while the pillars and ceilings are white marble, the symbol of serenity. It is the most expensive temple built in Gujarat to date. The intricacy of the carvings and decorations on its one central dome, twenty-five minor domes, and two hundred and fifty-eight pillars are a wonder to behold. It is a tranquil place surrounded by gardens, home to an enormous statue of Lord Shiva. It is a place to get lost in peaceful contemplation, where time races by unnoticed.

The temple of Shree Swaminarayan in Mandvi is just as opulent as all other Swaminarayan temples. It comes under the administrative control of Shree Swaminarayan Temple, Bhuj. The foundation stone was laid in 1991 on Samvat 2047, sixth day of Vaishakh by His Holiness Acharya Maharai Shri Tejendraprasadji, and Mahant Swami of Bhuj, and the temple was completed within eight years.

There are many majestic temples in India, the reasoning being that the grander the temple, and the grander the message, the less likely people are to turn away from God. Dad and I were of the school of thought that there were already enough temples to go around. If a town already had ten temples, why did it need another? Surely the huge amounts of money spent on building such opulent places could be better spent on constructing a new hospital, for example. At the end of the day, regardless of how grand a temple is or how many there are, nobody can actually leave God, so rather than concentrating on representing God, concentrate on doing God's work instead.

These opinions didn't affect the pleasure Mum, Dad, and their friends derived from visiting the Swaminarayan temple. The hours passed swiftly as they absorbed and admired the beautiful, peaceful surroundings. Before they knew it, their tummies were rumbling with hunger, and it was time to find something to eat. To their dismay, by the time they ventured back into Mandvi, it being only a small town, all the restaurants were closed. They searched and searched, until thankfully, they finally found a place on the second floor of a building that was still open. They hungrily feasted on piles of thick rotla (made from millet flour) smothered in makhana (butter), accompanied by chutneys, dahl, rice, and potato and aubergine curry. Glasses of cool spiced chaas went down a treat, and no doubt Dad had his fair share of any sweets on offer.

Revived and refreshed, the group then headed off to visit the Shyamji Krishna Varma memorial. This place was especially interesting to Dad as Shyamji Krishna Varma had been one of the foremost freedom fighters in the history of India's freedom movement, and Dad's knowledge of India's history, particularly regarding the fight against British rule, was extensive and impressive.

For over two hundred years, the British ruled over India, exploiting its economic resources and ruthlessly oppressing its people. Shyamji Krishna Varma was one of many individuals who took on the might of the British to free India, but he went a few steps further, taking the fight onto British soil and making his home in London.

Shyamaji Krishna Varma was born into humble circumstances in Mandvi, in October 1857. His father was a labourer for Cotton Press Company, and his mother passed away when he was only eleven, leaving him to be brought up by his grandmother. Nevertheless, he grew up to become one of the foremost freedom fighters in the history of India's freedom movement.

After graduating from Balliol College, where he was a noted scholar in Sanskrit and other Indian languages, Krishna Varma pursued a legal career for a short time before his move to London. He founded the India Home Rule Society and India House, which became an organised meeting point for radical nationalist Indian students in Britain, thus continuing the fight for independence from on the ground. His home in Highgate became a base for rationalists, free thinkers, and political leaders of India such as Lala Laipat Rai, Gandhi, and Lokmanya Tilak, and he published his own journal, *The Indian Sociologist*, through which he promoted the cause of India's independence through his and others writings. Krishna Varma believed strongly in the adage, "Resistance to aggression is not simply justified, but imperative." He became aware that the British secret service was closely scrutinizing his movements, so he quietly moved his headquarters to Paris before the British government had the chance to arrest him.

As Dad well knew, Shyamji Krishna Varma was not alone in fighting the cause for freedom. There were many other great radical Indian Nationalists committed to freeing their homeland from the vice of British rule. Many of them laid down their lives, both in India and abroad, to bring about their country's freedom.

The Shyamji Krishna Varma Memorial provided Mum and Dad with a glimpse into the life of this extraordinary man and his contributions to India's struggle for freedom. They were able to wander around the replica of the famous India House, the library, a research centre, and view paintings by renowned artists of other prominent revolutionaries. In the Smruti Kaksh of the Memorial, Mum and Dad saw the urns containing the ashes of Shyamji Krishna Varma and his devoted wife Bhanumati Krishna Varma. They strolled along the walk-through gallery, which displayed the timeline of how Shyamji's prepaid arrangements with the Geneva government saw his and his wife's ashes preserved at St. George's Cemetery, Geneva with instructions to send their urns back to India whenever it became independent during that period. After seventy-three years, Chief Minister of Gujarat State, Narenda Modi finally brought the urns of ashes back to Shyamji's birthplace, Mandvi.

Dad read every inscription, every nameplate, his face a picture of solemn acknowledgment of the sacrifices made to secure the freedom of his beloved country. It was cool inside the gallery, too, with its smooth marble floors and walls. A respite from the heat of the day, so when it was time to leave, Mum, Dad, and their friends felt revived and relaxed and ready to explore what the rest of the day had to offer.

SIXTEEN

"The Vedas are the source of true knowledge. To read and understand the Vedas is the supreme duty of one and all."

- *Swami Dayanand Saraswati*

The Vedas (meaning knowledge in Sanskrit) is a body of ancient texts or scriptures attributed to the sages of old. In the epic Mahabharata, their creation is said to be the work of Brahma (the god of creation).

In ancient India, before the British rule, the Vedas were taught to children in special residential schooling systems known as gurukuls. The teacher (guru) and students lived together in the same house or nearby and were considered equals. It was a sacred relationship, and no fee for the children's education was taken. Students usually attended the school from the age of nine to fifteen and saw nothing of their parents during that time.

A Vedic education emphasised the simplicity of living, with a strict schedule and respect for the teachers as central principles. Pleasure, comforts, and luxuries were unnecessary, with plain food, high ideals, and good behaviour encouraged.

Students learned about spirituality through prayer, yoga, and meditation. By cleaning up after themselves – washing dishes and clothes and making their own beds, they learned independence and the importance of equality. Vedic education teaches a way of life and develops a well-rounded personality through self-realisation, self-respect, and self-awareness. As well as teaching the students, the gurus also watched over their moral development and behaviour. Students were taught the importance of their duty to society and the world outside the school walls. Wealth was to be used for the good of society and not for their own wants. They were taught to respect all animals and plants and to value the importance of being good spouses and parents.

As well as being taught from books, students were also given vocational training in arts such as pottery and weaving and were taught the dignity of manual labour.

Much of the Vedas is dedicated to traditions, rituals, and cultures. The preservation of these is vital, so educating students in these areas was a way of passing down the traditions to future generations. Students were taught they owed three debts, one to the gods, one to past gurus, and one to their ancestors. Learning to serve the gods paid off the first debt, learning the teachings of past gurus paid off the second, and the third debt could be paid off by raising and educating their own future children in the ways of Vedas. In this way, traditions were preserved and passed on.

Central to the school's curriculum were the four Vedas – The Rigveda, the Yajurveda, the Samaveda, and the Atharvaveda - mantras or benedictions. The Aranyakas and Brahmanas texts, on rituals, ceremonies, and sacrifice, the Upanishads texts, which concerned themselves with meditation, philosophy, and the spiritual world, and the Vedangas, which consisted of six areas of study – Ritualistic knowledge, grammar, phonetics, metrics, astronomy, and the science of interpretation.

Various teaching methods include memorization, where students learn the sacred texts by heart through repetition and recital. Then there is introspection, which is a three-step approach. Firstly, Sravana, which is the listening to of texts recited by the teacher, then Manana, which involves deliberation and reflection. The third step is Nididhyasana, or meditation, through which the truth is realised and maintained. Critical analysis teaches the students to come to their own conclusions and even disagree with their teachers and bring them around to their way of thinking. Hands-on learning is encouraged for students who wish to enter various trades at a later date, and finally, seminars are held to encourage debates and discussions.

The schools placed an equal emphasis on body and soul

and on achieving spiritual enlightenment, so prayers and rituals were performed daily and at important milestones. Eligibility for the schools was not based on gender or caste, but every potential student had to undergo the sacred thread ceremony to become eligible.

When the British brought their influence to bear on India's education system during colonial rule, Vedic education gradually declined. However, in recent times, the value of this ancient form of education has seen renewed interest. Many privately funded gurukuls now exist in modern-day India, often run by religious trusts to bring back the philosophies of Vedic education. Mum and Dad's religious organisation, Swadhyaya Parivara, had opened a Vedic school in the small, century old town of Naliya. They headed here after leaving the Shyamji Krishna Varma Memorial in Mandvi, where they toured around the school and enjoyed hearing about its philosophies and successes. However, they weren't allowed contact with any of the students, of course. Naliya itself is a beautiful town with ancient Jain temples and mosques, which Mum and Dad saw in passing as they made their way to Amrutumliyam Mandir, built on a piece of land owned by Swadhyaya Parivara. While walking around this temple, they met a complete stranger named Vilubhai, also a member of their religious organisation. They fell into conversation with him, and he proceeded to invite them to his house for an evening meal. It proved to be a wonderful occasion, with another guest, Kana Rabani, filling the warm, evening air with bhavgeet (traditional devotional songs), of which he seemed to know an infinite number by heart. He sang for hours while Mum and Dad relaxed, enjoyed the company, and listened in bliss to the powerful yet soothing music. It was the perfect end to a perfect day.

SEVENTEEN

The Sanskrit word 'Prasada' or 'prasadam' means 'mercy,' or the divine grace of God.

Early the following day, Mum, Dad, and their little party set off for Narayan Sarovar, a village on the Kori Creek and a place of pilgrimage for Hindus. The sprawling lake that takes centre stage has great spiritual significance and is one of the five holy lakes of Hinduism; the others being Mansaovar in Tibet, Pampa in Karnataka, Bhuvaneshwar in Orissa, and Pushkar in Rajasthan. The origin of Narayan Sarovar dates back to the ancient Hindu religious texts, the Puranas. It is said that after there was a drought in the region, sages sent up desperate prayers, and Lord Vishnu appeared in response. Where he touched the land with his toe, a great lake sprang up, which saved the locals from their misery and thirst. The lake is one of the holiest lakes of Hindus and is sacred to Lord Narayan, an incarnation of Lord Vishnu. Many temples surround the lake, and it was to one of these, Shivji Mandir, that Mum and

Dad paid their homage.

From Narayan Sarovar, the group travelled to the tiny Swadhyaya Parivara village of Vandhai. Although there are only around seventy houses in the whole village with a population of 350 people, it is a place of huge religious significance for many Hindus. The ashram of Kutch's famous saint, Sant Shri Odhavramji is situated here along with the first Gurukul of Kutch, founded in 1937, and the Blind School, which opened in 1938. Mum and Dad visited Vashist Uparan Ruksh Mandir, which also encompassed a farm. After they had soaked up the spiritual atmosphere of the temple, they walked to the fields and helped themselves to ber fruit, coconuts, and handfuls of chikoo fruit, grown in abundance on the farm, satisfying their appetites with the fruit's soft, pulpy texture and sweet, malty, pear-like flavour.

Then it was time for the last stop-off of the day, the village of Mata no Madh, about an hour or so drive away from Vandhai. Mata no Madh is a beautiful village surrounded by hills and is home to the Ashapura Mandir, an ancient temple built in the 14th century dedicated to the Goddess Ashapura Mata. She is the Goddess who fulfils the wishes and desires of all those who believe in her, and is one of the principle deities of Kutch. Most idols of Ashapura Mata feature seven pairs of eyes.

Devotees by their thousands travel from Gujarat and other states to visit the temple on various auspicious days, such as Chaitra Navaratri and Ashvin Navaratri. On these occasions, camps and relief facilities are set up on the road leading to Mata no Madh to accommodate the large numbers of pilgrims.

A legend states that when the army of Mian Ghulam Shah Kalhoro of Sindh attacked the temple in 1762, the goddess Ashapura sent down a curse of blindness upon the soldiers. To negate the curse, Ghulam Shah swore to erect a huge bell in the temple. He kept his word, his soldiers regained their sight, and the bell still stands in the temple to this day.

Unfortunately, the mandir itself was closed on this particular day, but while Dad, Shamjibhai, and Keshavjibhai waited outside enjoying their fill of refreshing sugarcane juice, Mum and Ramaben managed to talk their way into the mandir. Not only were they able to view the shrine of Ashapura Mata with her image carved in six feet high red-painted stone (in years gone by, during the Navarati, the Rao of Kutch used to offer a sacrifice of seven male buffaloes at the base of the shrine), but they also received the food offerings, prasada, of puri, potato curry, and sweet meetha rice.

It was time to head home after an incredibly full day. Mum and Dad had savoured every moment and squeezed out every drop of enjoyment with their usual verve and stamina. No doubt the car was filled with the sound of their snores all the way back to Kutch.

EIGHTEEN

"Kutch nahi dekha toh Kuch nahi dekha!"

- *Amitabh Bachchan*

Day four saw the intrepid group of friends travel to Kalo Dungar or Black Hill; the highest point in Kutch, standing 462 metres high, and the only place to grab a panoramic view of the shimmering Great Rann of Kutch, the salt marsh in the Thar Desert reputed to be one of the largest salt deserts in the world. Because of its proximity to the Pakistan border, there is an army post situated at the top of the hill, only accessible by army personnel. The hill is known as Black Hill, not because of its colour, but because in times gone by, merchants returning to Kutch from Sindh would be guided across the desert by the black shadow cast by the hill with the sun behind it.

But the main attraction for Mum and Dad was the 400-year-old Datatray mandir at the summit. Legend has it that when Datatray walked the earth, he came across a pack of starving jackals outside the temple. Dismayed by their condition, he offered them his own flesh, which magically regenerated. Ever since, for the last four centuries, there is a unique custom whereby the temple priest prepares a serving of Prasad, cooked rice, to feed the jackals every evening after aarti.

Datatrey mandir is a small white and orange temple with several welcoming arches leading to the Sanctum sanctorum and the three-headed idol of Lord Datatreya. After wandering around the temple, Mum and Dad also perused the small shops outside, selling a variety of traditional dresses and Gujarati handicrafts. They didn't take advantage of the local vendors selling regional snacks of corn cobs, coconut water, and fruit juices as they had bought their own picnic of potato curry and thick rotlas, which they ate with plenty of butter while admiring the surrounding views.

Fortified by their meal, Mum, Dad, and their friends set off to their next port of call, to a place they had long dreamed of visiting. The Great Rann of Kutch is one of India's most treasured secrets. A place of mesmerizing beauty, this salt desert is around 7500km2 and lies a mere 10km from the Arabian Sea. The northern boundary of the Great Rann of Kutch forms the International border between India and Pakistan and is heavily patrolled by India's BSF (Border Security Force). It has long been the scene of perennial border disputes between India and Pakistan, and to acclimatize its troops to the inhospitable terrain, the Indian Army often conducts exercises here. The area was originally an outspread shallow of the Arabian Sea until a permanent geological shift closed off its connection to the sea. Over time the region became a seasonal, marshy, salt desert. During the monsoons, the marsh is submerged in seawater, which retreats in October, leaving behind a crunchy bed of salt. This mass expanse of cracked salt earth is breathtaking to behold, a white nothingness that stretches for miles that is unsettling and utterly stunning at the same time.

The region is home to the Kutchi people, who, living in an environment so lacking in colour, have become some of the most artistic people in the world. They embellish their clothes in sumptuous embroidery using the brightest yellows, blues, and reds, and their handicrafts are exquisite examples of mirror-worked garments, handmade footwear, and bead jewellery.

When Mum and Dad arrived, they stared in wonder at this great white desert shimmering in the sun before taking a ride in a camel-drawn cart over to a massive white metal viewing tower built to mimic the structure of a salt crystal. They climbed up three flights of steps, and once at the top, the view was mesmerizing, and they felt like mere dots amid the white vastness rolled out like an endless carpet under a perfect blue sky. They spent the rest of the afternoon here, and it was a wonder they had any energy left at the end of the day. But, of course, being Mum and Dad, it took only a night's sleep back at Keshavjibhai and Ramaben's house for them to be refreshed and ready for their next adventure.

NINETEEN

"One individual may die for an idea; but the idea will, after his death, incarnate itself in a thousand lives."

- *Netaji Subhas Chandra Bose*

The last month of the winter, February, is a hot month in Kutch, and Mum and Dad's final day there proved no exception. Mum chose her sari with care, wanting to look her best and keep as cool as possible while the sun shimmered with heat in the indigo washed sky. It was to be a day of pleasure for everyone. Mum would get to indulge in her favourite pastime and shop to her heart's content, while Dad would get to indulge his fascination in Mother India's Independence Struggle. And the place that would tick all these boxes was the Vande Mataram Memorial situated in Bhujodi, just outside Bhuj, a unique national monument and perhaps the only one of its kind in the world. Vande Mataram means Hail Mother/I bow to the Mother, and during the long and arduous freedom struggle between 1905 and 1947, the people shouted Vande Mataram first as a patriotic slogan and then as a battle cry. It became fashionable to shout "Vande Mataram" at Europeans and the police.

The memorial is a non-profit institution dedicated to immortalising India's journey to independence from British rule, from the revolt of 1857 until freedom was achieved in 1947. It is spread over twelve acres of land and displays, amongst other attractions, replicas of India Gate, the famous Parliament Building, and Yellow Fort. An amazing 4-D tour kicks off in the Parliament Building and takes visitors through a journey of thirteen episodes to relive the most historical moments during India's struggle for independence. The memorial was conceived and designed to relight the flame of patriotism and to help make the younger generation aware of the great sacrifices made by India's freedom fighters to win independence from British rule. Freedom fighters such as Shaheed Bhagat Singh, Mangal Pandey, Jawaharlal Nehru, and Mahatma Gandhi are all honoured through the 4-D episodes, which use synchronized special effects, art, and architecture to create a wonderfully immersive experience. Significant events in the struggle for freedom are all depicted, such as the British landing in the court of Emperor Jehangir, the Durban episode in South Africa, where Gandhi was unceremoniously off loaded onto the platform in South Africa, the Dandi March, the Quit India Movement, the martyrdom of Shaheed Bhagat Singh, and the transfer of power by the British to the Constituent Assembly of India.

Dad particularly enjoyed this experience and watched every episode with his heart filled with enormous pride and emotion. After this rousing exhibition, they explored the Yellow Fort, which houses an auditorium, an extensive library, a gallery dedicated to Gandhi, and a fabulous cafeteria offering a fine dining experience.

Surrounding the memorial complex are lush lawns to picnic on, relax, and contemplate the vast structure of the museum, which measures over 100,000 square feet and is modelled on the likeness of the Sansad Bhavan – the Indian Parliament building. Mum and Dad learned that it took over four years to build, with input from various prominent historians, sculptors, architects, and artists, the whole project initiated by the Ashapura Foundation.

The Ashapura Foundation was established to carry out cultural, social, and rural development in the Kutch district of Gujarat State. Kutch consists of around 900 rural villages and is known for its diversity of people, culture, and geography. But it lacks basic amenities such as water, power, and communication and is predisposed to earthquakes, droughts, famine, and cyclones. Most of the population of Kutch depend on agriculture and animal husbandry for their livelihoods, but rainfall is scanty, and no major rivers flow through the region. The development schemes began with the four most backward and inaccessible villages and quickly spread to over 101 villages.

The various projects implemented by the Ashpura Foundation include water harvesting, agricultural development, animal care, provision of drinking water facilities for animals, promotion of education, empowerment of people, creating employment for villagers, women and child care, relief and rehabilitation, and promotion and preservation of culture.

The grounds of the memorial also houses the Hiralaxmi Craft Park, another non-profit initiative by the Ashpura Foundation with a vision to preserve, restore and promote the arts of Kutch and to make them accessible to the public at large. The Managing Director of Ashapura Group, Mr Chetan Shah, came up with the idea after a group of rural artists were invited to the Ashapura guesthouse to demonstrate their artistic skills. He quickly realised that many of the art forms they displayed were on the verge of extinction due to a lack of funding and exhibiting venues. And so, the Hiralaxmi Craft Park was born, providing artisans with a platform to showcase and sell their wares along with free meals and lodgings during their stay at the craft park.

Mum strolled around gazing at every craft stall, shopping with her eyes, admiring the skill and workmanship in the beautiful embroideries, copper bells, Lippan art, Ajrakh printed fabrics, kala cotton saris, woollen shawls, and carpets. But, quite unlike Mum, she did not buy a single item. She didn't come away empty handed though, as Ramaben bought her a selection of sweets which she gifted to Mum in a traditional potla with a piece of cloth on top tied up with string.

The day ended with Mum, Dad, and their friends sitting in the memorial gardens watching the captivating and spectacular Laser Light and Sound Show projections on the Parliament House façade, which at sundown only added to a beautiful and somewhat surreal experience. To accompany the light show playing out before them, they dined on plates of delicious South Indian dosas rolled up and filled with spicy potatoes and vegetables, all served with a selection of tempting chutneys and sauces.

The whole day had been a delight, and this final evening ended their trip on a wonderful high. They travelled back to meet up with me again at Rajkot the next day, and to celebrate their return, my cousin's brother took us all out for one of India's most beloved of foods.

Pani puri occupies a special place in the hearts and stomachs of most Indian's. Go to any bustling market or busy main street, and the pani puri wala will be surrounded by an eager pack of hungry customers. The vendor will have to work hard, dipping the fried discs of dough (the puris) into various bowls of delicious fillings and chutneys before passing them over to all the impatient, outstretched hands. Everyone loves pani puri, from the richest to the poorest, and of all the fried snacks (chaat) the country offers, pani puri unites Indians in a unique way. Chaat – meaning to lick – is a word that encompasses a wide range of street snacks, where a multitude of ingredients are mixed together to create a sensation of tastes and textures. All of India love these snacks as they are the perfect solution to satisfy the hungry moments that pepper the time between lunch and supper. And pani puri is the star of all these snacks. It is soul food and a taste explosion in the mouth all at the same time.

Pani puri doesn't look particularly special. The word itself is a combination of pani (meaning water, specifically the special diluted chutney water used in this case) and puri, meaning fried discs of dough. The thin, crisp puris puff up when fried to create a hollow core, and this is when the delight and a touch of skill come in. You must poke a hole with your finger into the surface of the puri before then stuffing it with your favourite filling, which could be any type of spicy potato, chopped onions, smashed peas, or sprouts. Then dip the whole thing into sweet and sour tamarind and spicy chutney waters. Pop the finished parcel in your mouth and wait for the flavours to explode as the puri melts evocatively on your tongue. Watering eyes and juices dribbling down your chin are all part of the experience.

It is thought that pani puri originated from the northern

Indian region of Uttar Pradesh at the time of Emperor Shah Jahan's rule in the late 17th century. It is said that royal doctors recommended that the general population should eat more fried, spicy food and yoghurt to balance the alkaline quality of the water from the Yamuna River, where the new capital of Delhi was built. So the pani puri was born as 'bite-sized containers of the chaat masala,' and its popularity spread throughout the rest of the country by migrant workers moving into big cities.

Despite the fact that high-class restaurants have added pani puri to their menus with modern twists in their fillings and spiced vodkas shots instead of water chutneys, the snack is still at its best when enjoyed on the streets. Most pani puri vendors know their customers' preferences and modify the snack to individual tastes, adding more spice here or less chutney there.

We were no exception to the rule, and we gobbled down the delicious packages as we planned the next leg of our trip, one of the most meaningful and wished for, of Mum and Dad's whole stay in India. It was a trip they had been looking forward to doing their entire lives. And it was about to become a reality.

TWENTY

"He who has no attachments may definitely love others, for his love is pure and heavenly."

-   *Bhagwad Gita*

On 26th February 2019, we travelled by car (driven by the same driver as on the day of the accident) to the city of Junagadh, meaning 'old fort,' where we were to stay with the widow of Dad's cousin and her children Jigar and Amar for two nights. The ancient fortified city is situated at the foot of the Girnar Hills and has a history stretching back 2300 years. During the Partition of India and Pakistan in 1947, Nawab Mohammad Mahabat Khanji III of Junagadh chose to take his tiny state into Pakistan. It was a wildly unpopular decision, as the vast majority of the population were Hindus, so a plebiscite was called to decide the question of accession. India, in the meantime, cut off supplies of fuel and coal to Junagadh, severed air and postal links, and sent troops to the frontier. The nawab and his family fled to Pakistan when the plebiscite acceded

Junagadh to become part of the Indian state of Saurashtra until November 1, 1956, when Saurashtra became part of Bombay state. When Bombay state was split into the linguistic states of Maharashtra and Gujarat in 1960, so Junagadh became part of the state of Gujarat.

It is now a bustling city full of boisterous markets, gorgeous architecture, and a hugely welcoming population. It's also a great place to stay if you are visiting the lions at Gir National Park.

On our first day in the area, we rose early and set off for the tiny village of Laduli, the birthplace of my paternal grandfather. The village lies a short distance from the Gir Forest and has about twenty tiny houses to its name. Being so close to the forest and its population of Asiatic lions, it is not unusual for the villagers and the lions to come face to face. In fact, the day before our arrival, the villagers had chased off a pride of lions that had roamed too close for comfort. As a rule, the lions don't present too much of a problem, as, over the years, both humans and large cats have become accustomed to one another. The lions do not attack the humans, and the humans do not attack the lions. And if the lions ever do get too close for comfort, it is not unusual to see the villagers outside their houses banging together their pots and pans to scare the lions off.

As Gir Forest is a national park, it is patrolled by forest rangers, and these days the lions are tagged, so the rangers know exactly how many there are, and indeed, where they are. The lions have become something of a tourist attraction and are given a form of sedative to pacify them, which is a shame in many ways, as they are now not the wild animals they are supposed to be.

Dad had visited Laduli once before, as had I, but this was the first time Mum had been here. From my last visit, I remembered watching in fascination as the village women made rotlas in the traditional manner, stretching the dough with their hands clapping one on top of the other, turning 180 degrees with each clap, instead of using a modern-day rolling pin and cooking them on a flat tawa pan suspended over a small pile of burning sticks. It reminded me of cowboys making coffee out in the open in the old wild west. It was a lovely thing to see and warmed my heart to know some traditions never die.

Laduli is so small and rural that the electricity can go off at any given time. But unlike city dwellers who rely on this form of energy, the villagers of Laduli find it only an inconvenience when the power goes off. Theirs is a much more laid-back way of life. Before dawn, the village women rise from their beds to bathe, say their prayers, light the fires, and heat the water. Then it's time for the cows to be milked and the milk to be distributed to each house in the village. It's fascinating to see the lady going door to door with her large pan of warm, fresh milk, knowing just how many cups each family needs for the day. Unless there is a celebration of some sort where extra milk is needed, most people receive the same amount each day and settle their bills at the end of the month.

It was amazing to stand in front of the house where my grandfather was born; a tiny, two-roomed place that in his day would have had a traditional thatched roof but now has tiles. It was wonderful to share this moment with Dad and Mum and imagine my grandfather playing outside on the dirt roads as a young child. A magical moment came when Dad met his last surviving relative, who had the same great grandfather as himself. He and Dad even shared names. I was so happy that Dad got to meet this man, as I heard that he passed away not too long afterward.

My grandfather was born in Laduli in 1908, and he married my grandmother in 1925 when he was seventeen, and she was twelve. In those days, child marriages were extremely common (Gandhi himself and his wife, Kasturbai married at age twelve) until initiatives against them, bought in during colonial rule, saw the first law restraining child marriages passed in 1929. It was known as the Sarda Act and prohibited marriages of girls below the age of fifteen and boys below the age of eighteen.

When I thought about my grandfather's wedding, I often wondered how he and his entire village made the trip to my grandmother's village on bullock carts along dirt tracks in time for the wedding ceremony to take place and then for Grandfather to bring Grandmother back to Laduli. Luckily, my cousin Hiten, who lives close by in Malia, explained that wedding ceremonies in those days were three to four day events, including travelling, stopping over for meals and rest breaks at villages and houses along the way, while receiving the 'Athithi Devo Bhavo' attitude of Guests are Gods! How I wished I could have been a groom back in those days. I quite envied Grandfather that experience!

Back in the day, Grandfather used to own huge amounts of land just outside Laduli known as bighas. The bigha is a traditional unit of measurement of land commonly used in India, Bangladesh, and Nepal. There is no standard size of bigha, and it varies considerably from place to place. Grandfather's land wasn't worth anything in those days, so he never did anything with it. On my last trip to Laduli, when the head of the village realised who I was, concerns were raised that I had returned to reclaim my grandfather's land. By this time, people had built many illegal constructions on it to live in and had even tapped into the main electricity line. There was relief all around when I told them I had no interest in the land and certainly no intentions of turfing people from their homes.

The next village on our agenda was Bamnasa, the birthplace of my paternal grandmother. Growing up, my grandmother was the younger of two sisters with a gaggle of brothers in between. Consequently, she was spoiled and petted and blessed with a cheeky but feisty temperament — some of which most certainly got passed down to Dad and me. The school she attended still stands in the village, and it was here that we first headed. Family legend tells how my grandmother was expelled from this school for beating up the headmaster's daughter! Her education wasn't interrupted too much as she was married to my grandfather at the age of twelve, and as tradition dictated, went to live with him and his family. They, of course, slept in separate rooms until she was of an age to start marital relations. A few years later, when she was seventeen, she moved to East Africa with my grandfather, and it was there that Dad was born when my grandmother was twenty-four. It was fabulous to visit her old school and retrace her footsteps, imagining the mischievous girl she had been.

While at the school, we thought it was worth asking if the school archives still had a record of her school roll number. During the days of British rule, every schoolchild was issued with a unique roll number. We had the idea that if we could obtain this number, we would be able to prove our Indian ancestry and obtain an OCI- Overseas Citizen of India.

An OCI is a form of permanent residency available to people of Indian origin, allowing them to buy a property in India, register with banks, and live and work in the country indefinitely. In other words, it gives almost the same rights to Indians born abroad as those born in the country itself. The only thing OCI status does not allow is for the holder to vote in Indian elections or hold public office. Without an OCI, we can only stay in India for a maximum of six months, whereas with one, we could stay as long as we liked and only have to renew the OCI every fifteen years.

Because of Partition, when the country was split in two, a small part of Gujarat ended up in Pakistan. To prove our Indian ancestry, we would need to prove our ancestors were from the Indian side of Gujarat, and we thought obtaining my grandmother's school roll number would be the perfect piece of evidence. Unfortunately, we learned that due to mass flooding in the 1980s, the school archives were destroyed along with the hundred-year-old book that would have recorded my grandmother's roll number. So, it was not to be. But as that wasn't the main reason we had travelled to the village, we weren't too disappointed. We were only glad to have walked in the childhood shoes of my grandmother, together as a family, and to remember her famous exploits!

TWENTY-ONE

"Literacy in itself is no education. Literacy is not the end of education or even the beginning. By education, I mean an all-round drawing out of the best in the child and man-body, mind and spirit."

-   *Mahatma Gandhi*

The villages where my grandparents were born were all very close together, the bustling town of Keshod, south of Junagadh, being the epicentre of all four villages. It is said that during the time of Mahabharata, Krishna eloped with the beautiful, intelligent, and virtuous goddess Rukhmani when her brother Rukmi tried to force her to marry Shishupala. After hiding in the jungle for days and nights, Rukhmani washed her hair in the small pond nearby. In Sanskrit, Kesha means hair and Udd means to wash, and so the name Kesh-Udd, and what we now know as Keshod, came into being.

After visiting the villages where Dad's parents were born, it was now Mum's turn to visit the places her parents had been born. She had never been to these villages before, so it was with great excitement and anticipation that we set off to Kanjha, north of Keshod, the birthplace of Mum's father, or Bapuji as he was affectionately known. Bapuji's full name was Mohanlal Harjivan Raichura, and we were delighted to find the house he once lived in was now a temple called Raichura Temple. It filled Mum with a great sense of pride and peace to retrace her father's childhood footsteps, to breathe the air he once breathed, to see the sights he once saw, and to forge a connection with her roots. While at the temple, we got chatting with an elderly man who, to our amazement, not only knew Bapuji but had also met Bapuji's father Harjivan Hansraj Raichura. It was quite a mathematical conundrum to get our heads around, but we figured that if the elderly man had been a very small boy and my great-grandfather had been very elderly, then the meeting would indeed have been possible.

The elderly man was gracious and kind with a wonderful open smile, and he certainly didn't look his age. He was dressed simply in a threadbare, stained wrap, with a scarf around his shoulders, a wooden walking stick in his hand, and a friendly dog at his feet. His white beard was long to his chest, and his silver hair fell around his shoulders. It was such a fortuitous meeting, and we spent our time with him, laughing and listening to his stories, many of which we were already familiar with, so we knew the man was genuine. I captured these moments in a series of photographs, which I hoped Mum and Dad would treasure for a long time to come.

We visited the school that Bapuji attended as a child but were disappointed to find that the old school records had also been destroyed by the same floods in the 1980s that had wiped out my grandmother's school records, too.

The final stop off on our pilgrimage to my four grandparents' birthplaces was my maternal grandmother's village of Datrana, east of Keshod. The village is famous for being the birthplace of the Charan woman Nagbai who cursed Ra Mandalika III. The legend describes how Nagbaii was married to Charan Ravsur Bhasur and had a daughter-in-law named Minbai whose beauty was unrivalled.

One day, Mandalika came to the village. As custom dictated, whenever any great man visited a Cháran's village, the Cháran women would approach him face to face with a tray containing raw rice and kanku moistened with water. With the kanku they made the Tilak on his forehead, affixed some rice to it, then threw some of the grain or some flowers over him before blessing him and departing after cracking their fingers against their temples. When Minbai approached Mandalika to perform this ceremony, he turned away from her as he was so enamoured by her looks he was unwilling to accept her blessing as it would make her sacred from his unlawful desires.

Minbai didn't know what to do, so she ran to her mother Nagbai. "The Ra turned away," she said.

"Try him in another direction," suggested Nagbai. "Maybe there is a bad omen associated with him receiving a blessing in that direction."

So Minbai tried again, but still, the Ra turned away from her. "Mother," she cried. "I have tried all four directions, but he still turns away."

"You need not try anymore," replied Nagbai. "It is not Mandalika who turns but the days of his good fortune which have turned away from him."

As he was leaving, Mandalika placed his hand on Minbai's bosom. She ran screaming to her mother-in-law and complained of the insult the Ra had put on her. Nagbai then cursed him as follows:

The rule of the Rás shall pass away, and your sovereignty shall last no longer. A wanderer ye shall beg for alms and shall then remember me, Oh Mandalika.

The gate of the ancient fortress (Junágadh) shall fall;

You shall see the Damo Kund no more;

Your jewel shall be laid in the dust; And then shall you remember me, Oh Mandalika.

The descendants of Nagbai can still be found at Datrana, along with her shrine and memorial stone.

Just outside the village is a strange hill named Godhmo Hill, said to have once been the residence of a demon of the same name. At the hill's summit are small shrines dedicated to the goddesses Gatrad and Khodiyar, and the Rayan trees that cover the hill produce berries, that if taken away for private consumption, remain good to eat but if taken away to be sold will become rotten and filled with maggots.

We strolled around Datrana, so Mum could familiarise herself with her mother's birthplace before we headed to the school my grandmother had attended. We were surprised to learn that not only had my grandmother gone to this school, but my great-grandmother had also received an education there. It would have been unusual for a girl to attend school in my grandmother's day, let alone my great-grandmother's day. Under British rule, the education of girls was not encouraged, particularly as most girls married young. But it was also discouraged as a means of keeping the population uneducated and subjugated. So how did it come to be that my great-grandmother had gone to school? We thought the answer might lie in the forward-thinking innovations of certain Maharajas of the mid-nineteenth century, in particular the Maharaja Bhagvat Singh, who ruled Gondal, a small city in western Gujarat, from 1869 until 1944. Bhagvat Singh was the only Maharaja to become a medical doctor and a Fellow of the Royal College of Physicians of Edinburgh. He was also a lawyer and engineer, acquiring eleven different degrees during his lifetime and publishing the largest Gujarati dictionary and the first Gujarati encyclopaedia. After returning from his education abroad, he implemented an astonishing set of reforms and innovations intended to improve the lives of the citizens of Gondal. As well as abolishing all taxes, customs, and export duties, erecting hospitals, colleges, and schools, he introduced sewage, plumbing, rail lines, telegraphs, telephone cables, and electricity to Gondal. But one of Bhagvat Singh's most notable reforms was to make education free and compulsory for girls between the ages of seven and eleven in all villages of Gondal. If a girl did not show up to school for three consecutive days, he even sent officials to the girl's home to find out what was happening and, if he didn't receive a satisfactory explanation, he would demand that the girl be sent to school. Bhagvat Singh was an enlightened leader, and in his biography of 1934, he wrote that *"a girl's education had a social value that could not be exaggerated. She, in time, would bear children, and the children would be under her almost exclusive care during the most impressionable years of their lives. If she had attended school, they would imbibe education as they fed at her breast, or were dandled in her arms, or tugged at her sari as she went about performing her daily tasks. To educate a girl therefore, meant that a whole family would be uplifted; whereas to send a boy to school might conceivably mean that only a single individual had enjoyed the benefits flowing from the fount of knowledge."*

The Maharaja of Baroda State, Sayajirao Gaekwad III, was also instrumental in introducing many reforms during his rule from 1875 to 1939. The education of his subjects was one of his primary passions. He played a crucial role in developing many social and educational reforms, including banning child marriage, promoting ideological studies, religious education, and the fine arts, and being the first Indian ruler to introduce compulsory and free primary education in his state. His substantial personal library became the nucleus for the Central Library of Baroda, which grew to create a network of libraries in all the towns and villages.

Sayajirao was a charismatic figure and a visionary who passionately loved his country and people and harboured deep resentment and anger over British rule. He let his feelings be known publically at the majestic and historic imperial coronation ceremony at the Delhi Durbar in 1911, attended by George V, the first British monarch to travel to India, and where the Imperial Crown of India was created.

As an Indian ruler, Sayajirao was expected to dress in full regalia and perform proper obeisance to George V by bowing three times before him then walking away slowly without turning his back on the King. Not only did Sayajirao refuse to wear his jewels and honours, but he also refused to walk out backwards. Instead, he nodded perfunctorily at the British monarch, then turned his back and walked away in defiance. To this day, Sayajirao Gaekwad is a highly respected figure for having taken such a stance and for all the reforms he introduced to the state of Gujarart. It was fascinating to think that my grandmother and great-grandmother had benefitted educationally from the actions of Maharajas like Bhagwat Singh and Sayajirao Gaekwad. And to our delight, we found my grandmother's school still had all their records intact, so we were able to obtain the relevant paperwork to apply for an OCI for Mum. Once Mum was granted her OCI, Dad, myself, and my brother, as well as our future generations, would automatically get issued with one too.

I asked the school if I could give a donation but was told it was against the law to accept money from any sources other than official. "There must be something I can do," I asked. As it was late February and coming up to summer, I was told the school would be grateful to receive an electric water tank that would provide the children with cold water during the hot months to come. I was only too happy to agree. But little did I know that life had other plans for my family and me just five days later, and I am afraid that the children did not get their water tank that summer, although I have not forgotten my promise, and I will most certainly fulfil it as soon as I possibly can.

TWENTY-TWO

"Hell has three gates: Lust, anger, and greed."

-   *Bhagwad Gita*

After returning to Rajkot from my grandparents' villages, I took Mum and Dad shopping for outfits to wear to the much anticipated destination wedding in Jaipur that we were due to attend. Sonia, my cousin from my grandmother's side, was the bride-to-be, and she was thrilled that Mum and Dad had extended their trip to India to be at the wedding. The mother of bride-to-be had lived with Mum and Dad for a while when she first came to the UK, so she was especially fond of them and looked up to Dad as a father figure. The wedding was to take place in an ex Maharaja's palace, and whereas tradition usually dictated that the bride and groom were given the best room in the palace, on this occasion, to show the esteem in which they were held, Mum and Dad were to have the best room.

The bride and groom-to-be had also organised a tour of

Jaipur (known famously as the Pink City) for their guests to enjoy after the wedding, which Mum and Dad were looking forward to enormously. Every building in the historic walled center of Jaipur is a terracotta pink colour, and this colour is so essential to the heritage of the city that it is enforced by law. History tells us that the Maharaja of Jaipur was so determined to impress Prince Albert during his tour of India in 1876 that he first constructed a lavish concert hall named the Albert Hall in honour of the prince to ensure he would actually include Jaipur in his tour. The Maharaja then set about cleaning up and beautifying the dirty city, which included painting every building the specially chosen terracotta pink to represent welcoming and hospitality. The Maharaja's wife was so enamoured with the Jaipur Pink that she convinced her husband to pass a law making it illegal to paint the city's buildings any other colour. And the law still stands to this day.

With the upcoming tour of Jaipur in mind, alongside the wedding and the various celebration meals we would be attending, I determined that Dad would have something new to wear for every occasion. Being such a modest man, Dad only ever bought second-hand cars when he could have afforded Rolls Royces, and he only ever wore plain suits and ties when he could have afforded more lavish outfits. But this shopping trip was my chance to give him the best.

Before we set off for the shops, we were treated to a

fantastic meal at my cousin Lalo's house. His wife invited us at 10 o'clock that morning, insisting that it would be an honour to cook for us. By the time we arrived at the house, a mere two hours later, she had prepared a sumptuous meal that included two curry dishes, dahl, puri, vegetable rice dishes, ammras, and fresh mango for dessert. They were such a lovely family to spend time with, so warm and welcoming and modest. They had three daughters, and although they had little money, the father worked extremely hard to send his three daughters to private school. He doted on those girls and gave them everything he could, which was unusual as, in Indian culture, daughters are not usually prioritised. It was a wonderful thing to witness, and the occasion was made even more special as Dad's cousin from out of town also joined us for the meal.

Fortified by all the fantastic food, we finally made our way to the shops. I knew Dad would question the price of every outfit I chose for him, so I discreetly asked the shop assistants to remove the price tags before he tried anything on. But of course, Dad still couldn't stop himself from asking about the cost of every item. I told him a few white lies, pretending that something cost 10,000 rupees when in fact, it cost 30,000 rupees, and still, he was outraged. I can only imagine his reaction if he'd known the true price.

Dad was a naturally shy man who hated any kind of fuss. So I knew he was getting irritated by all the attention focussed on him as he ventured in and out of the changing room to show us how well the various traditional Indian items we chose for him fitted. Dad would never have dared to argue with the women, particularly his sister and her daughter-in-law Anuja, who had come on the shopping trip with us – that is not the Indian way. So he had to grit his teeth and bear all the fuss as his wedding outfits were decided upon for him. I bought him eight outfits altogether, and the one he was to wear for the actual wedding ceremony made him look so handsome we all joked he might get mistaken for the groom.

And of course, Mum, who had been resenting all the attention being showered upon Dad, got to have her turn in the spotlight too and left the store with a couple more gorgeous saris to add to her already 'Imelda Marcos' size collection.

With only a couple of days remaining before we left Rajkot to travel to Jaipur, my cousin came over all emotional thinking about our departure. He arranged to take extended family members and us out for a beautiful meal in an open-air restaurant unusually named Slurp With Salad.

The restaurant was just out of town, and the drive there was an adventure in itself, as the roads wove in and out of jungle-like scenery. We sat on the lawns and enjoyed a fantastic evening filled with laughter, family stories, and wonderful food. There was an all you could eat buffet which, as the restaurant's name suggested, offered a selection of mouth-watering salads, including Chinese salad, Mexican salad, Italian, Indian, and Thai. The ambiance was just perfect for a family occasion. At one point, my auntie, Dad's cousin's sister Vanita, became a little emotional at the thought of her brother's impending departure from Rajkot, wondering how long it would be before she saw him again. Little did anyone know how a tragedy would strike at the heart of our family just two days later.

As I watched Dad gently teasing his sister, admiring the easy, loving relationship they had, I couldn't help thinking about my brother and my children and how attachment to greed, lust, and the good opinion of others had driven our family apart. And my heart ached for all that was lost.

I thought about how my brother's jealousy over Dad's wishes to leave his wealth to me (and Mum's wish to leave her wealth to him) had driven my brother to inflict violence upon his own father. And I thought about how Mum's attachment to the good opinions of others had kept her silent and allowed the violence to continue. I thought about my ex-wife's mother and her attachment to lust, which she had passed down to her daughter; how it had devastated our marriage and how the lies that followed had left my children, my brother and his children hating me for all the wrong reasons. For a time, I had allowed myself to be the fall guy. As long as they are all happy, I told myself, what does it matter that injustice has been inflicted on me? I am just one person next to many.

Then one day, while watching the Indian epic Mahabharata, a switch had flicked in my head. Draupadi, said to be the most beautiful woman of her time, had married all five of the Pandava brothers – Yudhishthira, Bhima, Arjuna, Nakula, and Sahadeva - because of a mistake made by her mother-in-law. Yudhishthira's cousin, Duryodhana, chief of the Kaurava brothers, grew jealous of Yudhishthira and challenged him to a dice game. Yudhishthira accepted the challenge, but he lost at every turn, finally gambling away his own wife. After Yudhishthira lost Draupadi in the game, she was humiliated by the Kauravas and abused by Karna. The Kaurava prince Dushasana attempted to disrobe her, and only the divine intervention of Krishna saved her honour. Years later, in Kurukshetra, when all the soldiers of all the princely states gathered together to begin the great war, Draupadi asked Krishna if the humiliation of six people was worth the deaths of hundreds of thousands of soldiers: if it was worth the creation of hundreds of thousands of widows, and if it was worth the mass poverty that would follow. Krishna answered that if the war did not occur and the injustice was not righted, then future generations would believe that the way of unrighteousness had won and that it was okay to live an unrighteous life and do wrong, as no punishment would be forthcoming. So, for the sake of righteousness, the war had to be fought. And the war was fought, and many thousands of lives were lost, the only survivors being the five Pandava brothers.

Suddenly, as I watched the story of Draupadi being played out before me, I understood what I had to do. If my son and daughter and my brother's two children – my four candles – never got to hear the truth, never got to hear my side of the story, they would be living a life of lies. And future generations would grow up believing things about me that weren't true, so they also would be living a life of lies. I had to get my side of the story out there. Even if it meant more people would dislike me, and I became even more unpopular. For the sake of righteousness, I had to speak the truth.

My ex-wife was a wonderful woman in so many ways. She had a warm personality that attracted people towards her, and she was an amazing, caring mother and a fantastic cook. But when our marriage broke down due to her infidelity, she built a wall between my children and me, and that is her kalank – the dark stain on her character. There are only two ways to deal with kalank. The right way is to own up to your wrongdoing, to apologise and recognise the error of your ways. The wrong way is to deny any misdeed and to cover it up with layers of lies. But the truth cannot stay hidden forever. Truth is thinner than water, and it will always find a way out.

One of the best examples of how to deal with kalank, to my mind, is found in the life story of the 18th century slave trader John Newton. Born in 1725, Newton went to sea at a young age, working on slave ships. He eventually captained his own ships, continuing to carry goods to Africa to trade for slaves, who he shipped to the colonies in the Caribbean and North America. Conditions on board ships for slaves were appalling. They were packed below deck, chained together with leg irons, in spaces so cramped they were often forced to lie down or crouch. The lack of sanitation meant disease was rife, and fever, dysentery, and smallpox epidemics were frequent. Those who died were thrown overboard, and sometimes even if only one slave fell ill, the others chained to him would be thrown overboard to stop the spread of disease. The captives had to endure these barbaric conditions for up to two months, and as many as one in five did not survive the voyage.

In 1748, during his return voyage to England aboard the ship *Greyhound*, Newton had a spiritual conversion. He awoke to find the ship caught in a tremendous storm off the coast of Ireland and about to sink. He prayed for God's mercy, the storm began to die down, and after four weeks at sea, the *Greyhound* made it to port. The experience marked the beginning of Newton's conversion to Christianity. He renounced his trade, becoming a prominent supporter of abolitionism instead and an ally of William Wilberforce, leader of the parliamentary campaign to abolish the African slave trade. Newton openly apologised for "a confession, which comes too late. It will always be a subject of humiliating reflection to me that I was once an active instrument in a business at which my heart now shudders."

Newton's participation in the slave trade was his kalank – the scar on his character. But he acknowledged his wrongdoing and spent the rest of his life atoning for the part he played in such a brutal and horrific business. In later life, he wrote the hymn "Amazing Grace," and he lived to see the British Empire's abolition of the African slave trade in 1807, just months before his death.

"Amazing Grace, how sweet the sound
That saved a wretch like me
I once was lost, but now am found
Was blind but now I see.
Was Grace that taught my heart to fear
And Grace, my fears relieved
How precious did that Grace appear
The hour I first believed
Through many dangers, toils and snares
We have already come
T'was Grace that brought us safe thus far
And Grace will lead us home
And Grace will lead us home
Amazing Grace, how sweet the sound

That saved a wretch like me
I once was lost but now am found
Was blind but now I see
Was blind, but now I see."

In the Vedic way of life, we believe that John Newton will still face the karma of his cruelty. But as the cruelty returns to him, he will have spiritual strength and understanding due to the wisdom of his confession to make as good as possible on his wrongs. The good he did will also come back to him.

As I sat with my family that evening, with all these thoughts running through my head, I wished with all my heart that my ex-wife would acknowledge her kalank. I wished she would hold her hands up like John Newton had done, not for my sake, but the sake of our children and my brother's children, and so that any future generations would not be burdened with living a life of lies. Because those children had been fed a fiction throughout their years of growing up, and because they had been told that same fiction over and over and again, in their minds, this false version of events had become the truth. Say something long enough and loud enough, even to an adult, and he will believe it. Say the same things to a small child, and he will grow up believing what he has been told to be the gospel truth.

My four candles had become the victims of what is known as 'confirmation bias.' This is where one's beliefs and opinions are based on paying attention only to the information that upholds those beliefs while at the same time ignoring any information that challenges them. Sadly, this type of bias can prevent people from looking at situations objectively, influencing their decisions, and leading to poor or faulty choices. For example, in an election situation, people tend to look for information that shines a positive light on their favoured candidate and grasp information that shines a negative light on the opposing candidate. By ignoring objective facts and interpreting information in a way that only supports their existing beliefs, people often miss essential evidence and are blinded to the truth.

A shared fiction had been created, which was presumed to be the absolute truth. Reality was distorted to match this fiction, and the only person not involved in this fiction was the person they all thought guilty – me. Without a way to communicate with my four candles, they could not possibly get inside my head to know the absolute proven truth: the truth as proven by the DNA test, the truth established by Mum's video recordings, and the truth established by Dad's Letter of Wishes. And yet, even these absolute facts were, to them, fictional, and what was fictional, to them, was the truth. Their minds, ego, and confirmation bias would only permit them to turn a blind eye. Even those who knew the truth would never allow it to be verified. They only shout their lies louder.

I prayed so hard that one day my four candles *would* know the real me and that the mountain of lies would somehow crumble and the truth, like water, would find its own way out.

TWENTY-THREE

"What is thinner than water? – Knowledge of the Truth
What is heavier than the mighty Earth? – Sin
What is hotter than fire? – Anger
What is darker than kohl? – Kalank"

- *Anup Jalota 'Rang de Chunariya'*

Rang de Chunariya is a Hindu devotional song with deep meaning for Krishna devotees. A chunariya is an outer garment, a shawl or scarf, worn by females over traditional Hindu clothes. In the hymn, the word is used as a symbol to represent something entirely different. In Krishna Consciousness, the body is a covering, similar to a garment, and when we die, the soul discards the body and comes back in a new one, just as we would change our attire. So in the hymn *Rang de Chunariya*, chunariya symbolises the body, and the words translate as, 'paint my body.'

Anup Jalota, popularly known as the 'Bhajan Samraat,' a famous Indian singer, actor, and musician known for performing Hindu devotional music and bhajans, gave the best live rendition of Rang de Chunariya at the ISKON temple. The hymn is a beseechment from Meera, the celebrated Bhakti saint, and devotee of Krishna, asking God to paint her body (chunariya) in his colours. God is composed of infinite colours (wisdom), so asking him to paint your body in his colours is extremely desirable for Krishna devotees as it includes heart, mind, and soul. Meera states that she doesn't want just any colours, she wants the exact colours of God, and they should never be washed off so she will never forget the wisdom.

Rang de chunariya...
Paint my body...

Shyaam piya, mori rang de chunariya.
Oh Lord, (please) paint my body.

Aisi rang de, ke rang nahi choote,
Paint it such, that the colours never come off,

dhobiya dhoye chahey, ye sari umariya.
even if the laundry-men wash it all of their lives.

lal na rangavu mei,
I do not want red,

hari na rangavu,
I do not want green,

Apne hi rang me, rang de chunariya.
Paint my body in YOUR colours.

Bina rangaye mai to, ghaar nahi jaoongi,
Without (god's wisdom) colours, I will not go home,

biti he jaaye chaahe, yeh sari umariya.
even if it takes my whole life.

Mira ke prabhu, Giridhar Nagar,
Mira's says, "Lord Giridhar Nagar",

(Questions)

Jal se patla kaun hai?
What is thinner than water?

Kaun bhumi se bhari?
What is heavier than earth?

Kaun agan se tej hai?
What is hotter than fire?

Kaun kajal se kali?
What is blacker than kohl?

(Answers)

Jal se patla gynan hai,
Thinner than water is knowledge of the truth,

aur paap bhumi se bhari.
(and) sin is heavier than earth.

Krodh agan se tej hai,
Anger is hotter than fire,

aur kalank kajal se kali.
(and) shame is darker than kohl.

Mira ke prabhu, giridhar nagar,
Mira's says, "Lord Giridhar Nagar",

Prabhu charanan me,
At Prabhu's (Lord's) feet,

Hari charanan me,
At Hari's (God's) feet,

Shyaam charanan me,

At Shyaam's (Krishna's) feet,

Lagi najariya,

With a fixed gaze,

Shyaam piya, mori rang de chunariya...

Oh Lord, (please) paint my body (in your colours).

This devotional hymn resonated deep in my soul. The four questions asked and the four answers given were so pertinent to my life. No matter how deep the truth is buried under a mountain of lies, it will find its way out, whether in this life or the next, and the weight of sin cannot be carried forever. That anger is hotter than fire is where I went wrong in my life. Every time I found out that Sia had been unfaithful to me, I reacted with anger. And when I found out that my daughter was not my own, I again reacted with anger. That anger did not serve me well. My anger at my situation turned my righteousness into a wrong. It turned my whole world upside down.

My anger at the wrongs done to me was turned against me. My children believed that I had been unfaithful to their mother, not the other way round. My daughter accused me of lying about the DNA test results, which proved she was not my biological daughter. But yet, when I offered to arrange for another test to be done, after first agreeing, she never followed it up. To me, this could only mean that she knew I was telling the truth but had chosen to keep the proof buried to protect her mother. When I tried to visit my son at university, he refused to see me, believing all the falsehoods his mother had told him. Before I knew it, I was taken to court, accused of harassment. The ensuing court case was one of the most harrowing things I had ever experienced. The truth was twisted, distorted, and buried alive under an immense weight of falsehoods, fiction, and misrepresentation.

When my daughter took the stand, she seemed to have forgotten all the happy times we shared and all the things I did for her as a good father. I have many videos of our two glorious family holidays in Florida, of my son's Mundan when he was two years old, where my seven-year-old daughter is sitting on my lap, and my son is taking Smarties from between my lips with his lips. How had my daughter forgotten these things? I have a video of my daughter and me playing chess together, as we often did. When she found it hard to fit in at her new school, I let her win these chess games, thinking it would help build her confidence and see herself as a winner and not a loser. It was my way of wiping away her tears and helping her to feel good. Had she forgotten these things?

That day in court, she downgraded all the happy times we had shared. She spoke about me as if those times had never existed, and her words tore my heart to shreds. For her happiness, I was prepared to walk behind her, so she felt in the lead. Now she has left me so far behind and never wants to look back. I was the only fool to have her in my prayers and blessings more and more. I prayed that she moved far ahead in her life and succeeded in everything, including hating me and leaving me further and further behind if it made her happy. Her hating me became a good thing for her. If kids' lives are broken into two by their parents dividing, then they become divided too. By hating me and loving her mother, at least my daughter remained whole and not broken into two.

My son's written statements to the court portrayed me as a less than good man who cheated on his mother. I had never lifted a finger in violence, although I had been overcome by anger on many occasions, particularly when I received the DNA results which proved my daughter was not mine. I realised, listening to my son's words, that he still believed it was me who had cheated on his mother, and no one had told him the truth regarding the DNA results. Due to a case of mistaken identity some time ago, I had also been charged with drink-driving. Although the charges were later revoked, my son didn't know this and still believed I was a drink-driver. As I rarely touched alcohol, this was a particularly harsh judgement for me to bear.

The whole court case was designed to prevent the truth from reaching my son and for my daughter to protect her mother and keep the web of lies intact. Their intent proved successful, and without being allowed to defend myself against the allegations in a second hearing, an injunction was served, which forbade me to contact my son directly or indirectly for the foreseeable future. A heart could not have been more crushed than mine.

Even my brother's two children have forgotten all the occasions I would bring them back toys from my work trips to Europe. The youngest won't remember when I comforted him after his mother accidentally dropped him from his baby sling in Richmond Park. And do any of my four candles remember how I used to make them laugh with my silly magic tricks?

I have all the evidence needed to back up the truth of everything. My anger was the only thing that made me wrong, and I have been severely punished for it. Not only by the people who want my proven truths to be considered insignificant and lies, out of fear that the truth will shine a light on the real culprits, but also by those who started to believe these lies. My son's happiness was not taken away by me as much as it was by his mother's attachments to men. And my nephews' innocence has been destroyed by being sold lies from a very young age by those who face humiliation from the truth coming out. Yet, they will be happy living a life of lies and be adamant that it is the truth. They will never have the courage to challenge what they have told for fear the lies are exposed. They and their future spouses and their children and all future generations will have to live the life of cowards as well as a life of lies.

TWENTY-FOUR

"Each one has to find his peace from within. And peace to be real must be unaffected by outside circumstances."

-   *Mahatma Gandhi*

Our evening at the restaurant Slurp with Salad finally wound to an end. The easy conversation, love, and respect between us all had been a salve to the soul. When we returned to Vishal's house, I was not quite ready for the day to end. I wanted to hang on to the very last threads, and so after saying goodnight to Mum and Dad, I sat under a street lamp with Raghuraj, the guy next door, and indulged in a game of chess which had been my habit for a few nights now. It was wonderful to have the peace of the night to ourselves, to have only the inky sky, the soft yellow glow of the moon, and the brighter flashes of starlight for company. The only unwelcome guests were the whining mosquitoes who feasted on my ankles and the back of my hands.

The next day we went on another family outing to an

amusement park. It was a day for the kids, a day for my little nephew to use up all his energy running around testing out all the rides and for us adults to have just as much fun watching him. The conversation, easy teasing, and banter flowed over fizzy drinks and delicious street food. There was much laughter and a sense of squeezing out every last drop of joy from being together as a family, knowing that Mum, Dad, and I would be leaving the following day.

Later that evening, Mum found me talking with Vishal outside. She joined us, and when Vishal went back inside the house, she took her opportunity. "Mayur," she said. "I am sorry. I will try and talk to Arjun. I know doing this will anger your brother, but I need you to stop shouting and yelling at me from now on."

I was humbled and heartened by Mum's promise. "Mummy," I said. "Nothing will make me happier than to have my devotion back for you. I guess we will have to work hard to earn back each other's love and respect." I took her hand. "But Mummy, you need to stop lecturing Papa, too. Forgive him for your hurt in the past, and I know I need to stop shouting at you." I sighed and looked down at my feet. "You know, don't you, Mummy, that Arjun has been brainwashed to never believe anything nice about me? He will swear any proof otherwise is fabricated. Even if the DNA test was taken in front of him, he would not believe it. You will push him away from yourself by speaking to him, but I guess you will have to pay for this and make it up in your next life, as will Arjun and I."

I looked up and smiled sadly at Mum. "Oh, Mummy. You always had the knack of making me angry. Anger is the weakness of our family. My brother would always raise his hands to Dad, and I would shout and lose my temper, but never physically. Do you remember?" I said. "How as a child everyone called me Mavadyo? I was so proud to follow you around. I thought you were the best and prettiest mother ever. Even when Papa made his one big mistake, I was destroyed on the inside from seeing the hurt in your eyes. I was so angry at him. When you and Papa fell out, you would come and stay at my house. And the final time you came, you exposed our cracks to the world because you wanted attention. I felt the whole world, especially my brother and his wife, saw a massive opportunity. Poor Papa lost his grandchildren on that day after he was told to choose between them or me. It reminded me of the evil Sakuni misleading the innocent and wise of Mahabharat. But when you had the opportunity to seal the cracks between my children and me, you couldn't do it because you feared your grandchildren would shun you like they did Papa. You may not see this, but Papa's wrongdoings decades ago dwarf your wrongdoings ever since. This pride I had in you, the feeling of devotion, vaporised into pity and anger."

Neither of us noticed Dad come outside to join us until

his voice interrupted. "The fault is not entirely your mother's," he said. "I did the wrong thing, and I live with regrets every day." He looked at me. "It was me who clipped your wings by allowing your brother to control your life. In the last ten years, I realised just how high you could fly with what you have achieved in your property business. If I had let you take to the skies your way and stopped your brother controlling you, your success would have been unparalleled. Your brother's life income achievements are nothing compared with what you have done in a decade. The only reason he flies high is because of the massive wealth I gave him. It is also my fault that he has become violent. I planted the seeds when you two were young. When he was growing up, I treated him more favourably than you. Now you have the right to laugh at me. You have the right to say to me that your favourite son is a violent thug."

It was Mum's turn to interrupt. "Why do you never have anything nice to say about him? He is your son."

"Because he is a violent thug," Dad said to her. "You have witnessed his violence towards me. That is why I have disclosed this in my Letter of Wishes. In the eyes of everyone, they only see his righteousness. He never shouts and yells like Mayur. He waits for the opportune time when no one else is there. And he knows you will keep quiet."

I turned to Mum and said, "Mother, the truth is that I want you to come with me to India for at least a month every year.

It will get you away from winter in the UK, too. I want to travel from Ladhak to Kanya Kumari and see the varying wonders of this great country. If you come in December and January, I will take you to South India. If you come from March to May, we can explore the Himalayas, Ladhak, Himachal, and the remote northeast. We can even do the Char Dham yatra. If you come in October and November, we can see even more of our beloved Gujarat and all of middle India from Calcutta to Bangalore to Maharashtra and Rajasthan."

At this point, Vishal came back outside and caught the end of our conversation. "Yes," he said. "Our India is truly an amazing and magical country."

As Mum, Dad, and Vishal continued talking about their beloved country, I sat back and tried to absorb the conversation that had just taken place. Certain truths dawned on me that made me feel ashamed. In the Indian tradition, a son sees the whole world, heaven and God, at the feet of his parents. I realised then that my brother and I had failed. My brother had failed with Papa, and I had failed with Mummy. Their sons, their own flesh and blood, were stained with shamefulness. Our living Gods had witnessed themselves becoming trivial and insignificant in the unappreciative minds of their sons. Sons should be their parents' walking sticks in later life, whom they can rest on for happiness and strength to walk further. Whether the parents need their children to be their walking sticks or not, as sons, we should have needed to be our parents' walking sticks, as heaven is in serving them. We had truly failed. We had truly hurt our parents. When parents sacrifice everything for their children when they are growing up, it is seen as the parents' duty. When the same children have to sacrifice just a fraction to take care of their parents in their old age, it is seen as a favour the parents have to beg for. Children are never seen as a burden, but in old age, parents are seen as a burden to the same children who should be serving their living Gods. Shame on my brother and me, I thought. Parents forgive their children from the heart, no matter the seriousness of their child's misdemeanour. But parents have to beg for forgiveness or face punishment. And sometimes violent punishment whether they were wrong or not. The knowledge that my brother and I had acted so badly towards our living Gods hit me hard and filled me with shame. I realised that my ego had never allowed me to see this before.

But at the same time, I was filled with joy that Mum had finally done something mahan (great righteous) for me. I had waited endlessly for this moment. For so long, Mum had wanted people to call her saras (wonderful) and see her as mahan. Now she had apologised and promised to risk sticking her neck out to get my son, Arjun, back with me. She had let go of the idea of wanting to be liked and be seen as mahan. And because of this, in my eyes, she *became* mahan. At that moment, I felt true devotion for her. At her feet, I once again saw the heaven and God I was seeing at my father's feet. It was the realisation I needed. All of a sudden, I was filled with self-pride again, and my self-respect soared to its peak.

TWENTY-FIVE

"Parents are living Gods. Learn to respect them. Without their blessings you will not get life's blessings."

-   *Kavi Ram*

The day had come for Mum and Dad to leave Rajkot after a wonderful month taking in the sights, sounds, tastes, and smells of their beloved India. It had been an honour and a joy for me to have arranged everything for them, so all they had to do was relax and soak everything up. That we had met and reunited with so many family members had been deeply meaningful, and we felt blessed, humbled, and thankful for everything we had experienced.

Before travelling to the wedding in Jaipur, Dad wanted to head back to Vadodara to sort out some business affairs regarding a property he owned there. In their India Will, Mum and Dad had stated that the property was to be left to me as my brother had no affiliation to India. The original plan was for Mum and Dad to take the bus, but I couldn't countenance the thought of the two of them having to manage all their luggage by themselves, then having to sort out a rickshaw once they reached Vadodara. Would Mum's luggage even fit in a rickshaw?! Dad would most likely get ripped off by the autowalah, and then Mum would have to cope with Dad being grumpy and angry...so, no. I decided I couldn't allow them to travel alone and told them I would be accompanying them on the trip and booked a car to take us.

We all ate a hearty breakfast to fortify us for the day ahead, after which I made sure that Mum and Dad had packed all their belongings as they would be flying back home after the wedding. I only took one bag with everything I needed for the wedding and left the rest of my stuff at my cousin's house, as I would be heading back to Rajkot once the wedding celebrations were finished.

After a teary and emotional farewell to our family, we set off for what should have been a perfunctory diversion before we headed to the exciting main event in Jaipur. Mum and Dad sat in the back of the car while I rode in the front next to the driver. The driver wasn't a stranger to us as we had used his services before, so we all settled down and relaxed into what was going to be at least a five hour journey. For the first hour or so, we chatted lightly, passing comments and jokes to one another from the front to the back of the car and vice versa. The driver was a young man in his twenties, and I was irritated to notice he had the same habit of playing with his phone as he had the last time we had used his services. On that occasion, I had let it go and hadn't pulled him up on his dangerous habit. But now, he was driving along the highway at great speed with his phone in his hand, and I felt increasingly uneasy. I reached out and took the phone from his hand, telling him we would stop at the next eatery on the highway to grab some food and fizzy drinks, and while we were there, he could play with his phone to his heart's content. "But, please leave the phone alone while you are driving," I asked him.

He apologised, and as I settled back in my seat, I caught Dad's eye in the rear-view mirror. He was nodding and smiling as if to say, *"Thank you, Mayur, that was the right thing to do."*

Before long, the rhythmic motion of the car began to make us all feel sleepy. Mum's head nodded, and her eyes slowly closed. But it was then that she murmured the words my heart had been longing to hear.

"From now on, your father and I will come with you to India for one month every year."

After all the anger, bitterness, and sadness of the last few years, it felt like my living God had finally come back to me, and I was filled with a beautiful warm feeling, a mixture of love, gratitude, and contentment. Mummy and I had found closure, and I couldn't have asked for anything more. Papa and I grinned at each other, and Mummy, through closed eyes, told us off for laughing at her, and then we all drifted off into a light sleep, with the noise of blaring horns – a feature of Indian drivers and highways – fading into the distance.

Suddenly, the shrill ringing of a phone jolted me from sleep. I lazily opened one eye to see our driver taking a call. I was happy to note he had taken my advice, and the phone was on hands-free, so I closed my eyes again to enjoy another little snooze. A few minutes passed, and I became aware that the sound of a hooting horn was coming from right next to me. I kept my eyes closed, thinking our driver was just hooting at someone he wanted to pass. Then suddenly, a deep blaring horn sounded to my left, and my eyes shot open as I looked around to see what was going on.

What happened next is like a scene from a horror movie. When I picture the events in my mind, everything happens in yawning slow motion. We are in the right-hand lane, and our driver is beeping at the car in front of us, impatient to pass it. The car tries to move into the left-hand lane, but there is a fast moving truck in the way that sounds a warning blare. The car swerves back into our lane, but our driver has accelerated by now, and my mind registers that we are heading for a collision. I turn my head to see the phone in the driver's hand. Then, with sickening force, our car smashes into the central reservation. The world turns upside down. My stomach fills my mouth. The car rolls over and over, and the image of my son floats in front of my eyes. Arjun! I cry. Arjun! And then I am spat from the car and smashed onto the tarmac.

I open my eyes, and there is the sky again. But I don't want to see the sky. I try to turn my head to one side. Slowly, slowly. It hurts so much.

I see her. I see them. I see Mummy lying on the ground close to me. She is so still. Is she still sleeping? I stare at her eyelids, willing them to flicker. I stare at her chest. Is it moving? I wait for the silk of her sari to shift as she takes a breath. But there is nothing.

I look at Papa lying next to her, and my heart clenches. He is looking back at me. Our eyes meet, and it is like he has taken me in his arms. He is smiling, his gentle, beautiful smile, and I dare to hope he is ok.

But then he is not looking at me anymore, even though his eyes are still open. The light has gone out. With his familiar smile still laid peacefully on his face, he drops his head, and I know that he, too, has gone.

The world turns into a confusion of pain, and noise, light, and darkness. I think of Papa and how he was one in a hundred million because he was born with his heart on the right side of his body, a condition known as dextrocardia that affects less than one percent of the general population. The phrase, 'his heart is in the right place,' was especially true for him. He was the most kind-hearted, generous soul you could ever wish to meet. He would have given the clothes off his back if he thought it would help anyone.

Pain has numbed my mind. I cannot process the thoughts that run riot through my brain. I know there's been a car accident. I know my living Gods are lost, but I cannot feel the impact of any of this. It is a nightmare that is happening to someone else. It is a nightmare that I cannot wake up from.

Paramedics lift me onto a stretcher, and white hot pain takes my breath away. I don't know where the pain is coming from or what has happened to my body. As they carry me away from the scene, panic grips me. "No!" I scream. "I am not going anywhere without my parents!" I struggle to climb off the stretcher, but I cannot seem to move my legs. "Please!" I scream. "I don't want to leave them."

One of the paramedics leans down to me. "They are no more," he says gently. "We have to go."

"Please," I beg. "Just give me one minute. Just one last minute with them."

My wish is granted, and I stare down from the stretcher at my two living Gods lying so motionless on the ground. I cannot comprehend that they are lost to me when, what seems like only moments ago, we were teasing each other in the car, dozing like babies, and my heart had been filled with contentment knowing that Mum and I had found closure with one another. I had just spent thirty days in Heaven with them, and now this is the last time I would ever see them. From now on, I would only ever see them in my dreams and memories.

Voices babble over my head as paramedics slide my stretcher inside an ambulance and close the door. The ambulance rattles at speed along the highway, and I reach out my hand to hold onto the side of the vehicle, knowing that if I don't, I will be flung to the floor. I stare at the blood on my hand, wondering where it has come from. When the ambulance finally stops, the doors are opened, and I am trundled on the stretcher into the belly of a government hospital, where I am left on a trolley in a corridor. The stillness is welcome, but only for a moment. Through searing pain, I see that final smile on Papa's face again. The smile that said, despite the agonising pain he was suffering, he was happy to see his son alive. When his head finally dropped, that beautiful, beautiful smile was still on his face. The only man I ever knew who smiled his way to death. The only man I ever knew whose heart was big enough to encompass all those he loved and even those who did not love him. The only man I ever knew whose heart was so big that all Mum's eight siblings and many on his side of the family benefitted financially from his rise from rags to riches. Yet, he led a very simple life. When he could have afforded a brand new Bentley, he was happy with a second-hand Japanese car and instead gave his children generous deposits to buy properties and made sure his grandchildren did not have student loan debts. But even this generosity was dwarfed by the generosity of time that he gave to everyone, particularly towards spirituality and the uplifting of others. To me, my Papa was comparable in generosity to Karna from the Hindu epic Mahabharata, and equal to Arjun in his steadfastness and dedication, courage, strength, and humility.

And now, his shining light had been extinguished. But only in this world. His light and Mummy's light would shine forever in my heart and the hearts of everyone's lives they touched.

TWENTY-SIX

"I have a purpose for your pain, a reason for your struggle, and a reward for your faithfulness. Trust me, and don't give up."

- *Lord Krishna*

As the ambulance sped me to the hospital, my phone began to ring. The paramedic fished it out of my pocket and held it to my ear. It was my cousin Vishal, and hearing his voice sent fresh waves of emotion coursing through my broken body. "What has happened Mayur? What has happened?" his voice was shrill with concern and panic. He explained that someone at the accident scene had found Dad's phone and had pushed last number redial. They had reached Kantibhai, a member of Swadhyaya Parivara, who had in turn called Vishal. "Where are you?" he asked me. "Where is the ambulance taking you?"

I did my best to answer his questions while waves of pain made me groan out loud. I was vaguely aware of Vishal telling me to hold on; he would meet me at the hospital and sort everything out.

My phone rang again. When I heard the voice on the other end, I almost cried out loud. It was my brother - the brother who had not spoken to me for years. The brother who I had thought had no feelings left for me. "Mayur. What has happened? What has happened?"

Through my pain, confusion, and fear, I managed to tell him about the accident and what had happened to Mum and Dad.

"Don't worry," he said. "I'm coming. I love you. Nothing is going to happen to you."

Was this really my brother speaking to me? The brother I thought I had lost forever? The brother who had shown no emotion towards me for years? His voice shone a light through the darkness. It was something for me to cling onto as the ambulance sped me away from the bodies of our parents towards a life I now thought would have no meaning.

As I lay on the trolley in the hospital corridor, drifting in and out of consciousness, I became aware of another man's cries of pain. I looked down, and there, lying on a stretcher on the floor, was our driver. My heart went out to him. His tear-filled eyes met mine, and I saw the guilt and pain etched across his face. "Don't worry. Everything will be fine," I tried to reassure him. "Everything will be okay."

When the doctors came to help me, I asked them to look after him first, but my pain became overwhelming, and the world faded away again. When I next opened my eyes, Vishal was by my side, explaining that he had organised an ambulance to take me to a private hospital. He travelled beside me all the way, holding my hand and telling me I would be okay and not to worry. His face grew blurry, and his voice seemed to come from far, far away. Somewhere deep in my consciousness, I realised I had been sedated, and I sank with relief into oblivion.

Time lost all meaning. On the occasions I opened my eyes, I had no idea where I was. I was aware of bright lights, low voices, and the concerned faces of nurses looking down on me. Other times, I was more lucid, and the shock of everything hit me again, harder and harder each time. It was impossible to believe that Mum and Dad, my living Gods, were truly gone.

My cousin Mitesh arrived, all the way from London, to be by my side. As a highly respected dentist with close contacts in the medical profession in Rajkot, Mitesh knew the doctor treating me, Dr. Sanjay. He used his position to persuade the doctor to change my medication to reduce my pain. Although the new drug's side effects would cause me to hallucinate, Mitesh joked that there was good news and bad news. "The good news is, you will not remember the pain you are in. The bad news is, the drugs will make you hallucinate. But that is normal for you," he laughed. "That is the way you live your life."

He was right about the hallucinations. The following days were filled with strange dreams, voices, and smells. People visited me who weren't really there. Sometimes the hallucinations were terrifying, and sometimes they were welcoming. But at least I couldn't remember the horrific pain, and my screams diminished. At one point, I was sure my brother was in the hospital room with me. At first, I dismissed him as a vision, a figment of my hallucinations. But after a while, I realised to my intense joy that he was solid flesh and blood. That my brother had flown five thousand miles from London to be with me meant the world at that moment.

More family members arrived at my bedside. My cousin Krish, from Mum's side, flew in from the UK. My cousin Hiten from Malia, and another cousin Ashish, also travelled from the UK to be with me. But instead of coming directly to the hospital, Ashish went first to Virpur and the temple of Jalaram Bapa.

Jalaram Bapa, popularly known as Bapa, was a Hindu saint born in Virpur, Rajkot district, Gujarat, in 1799. He is worshipped throughout Gujarat, but his wise words and miracles have spread across India and many other countries. Images of Bapa show him wearing simple white clothes to represent purity while carrying a tulsi mala in his right hand and a stick in his left. He was a devotee of the Hindu god, Rama, and is well known for founding 'Sadavrat,' a feeding centre, where sadhus, saints, and the needy could find food at any time. Devotees of Jalaram Bapa know that if they pray sincerely to the saint, he will bless them and fulfil their wishes. These experiences are known as Parchas.

Dad was a huge devotee of Jalaram Bapa, as were many other members of both Mum and Dad's families. So, with this devotion in his heart, my cousin Ashish visited Jalaram Bapa's temple in Virpur to pray for me and bring back offerings. When he arrived at my bedside, he presented me with a small statue of Jalaram Bapa along with a flower presented at the feet of Jalaram Bapa in Virpur that he placed under my pillow. In 1970, in Tanzania, Ashish's father, Jayanti Vithlani, was given up for dead after robbers had violently beaten him. A lady from the village of Karumu, where Mum was born, had given Ashish's mum a similar flower offered with a sincere prayer to place under his pillow. Not only did Ashish's father survive, but he lived to tell the tale for another 35 years.

Ashish comforted me. "Mayur," he said. "Nothing is going to happen to you. Bapa is with you now. And your parents are with Bapa." He leaned down and kissed me on my forehead, as did my cousin Hiten.

Then, most consoling of all, my brother, too, leaned down and kissed me on the forehead. "I love you," he said. "I'll make sure nothing is going to happen to you. I will look after you and take you home. I will do that for you."

On hearing my brother's words, an immense peace descended on me. I was in a critical condition, with multiple injuries, and there was little hope that I would survive. But amid my pain and delirium, I heard my brother's voice, and I remembered the brother he had once been. I remembered the brother who had spent his first wage packet on three leather jackets: one for himself, one for my cousin, and one for me. I remembered the leather jacket he gave me cost more than the jacket he bought for himself. And I remembered the time I was away at university in Wales, and my brother heard cold weather was on its way. A parcel arrived for me one day, and inside were two woollen jumpers, one green, one blue, and a note saying, *keep warm, brother*. I was so proud and happy to have such a thoughtful, loving brother, and every time I wore the jumpers, it felt as though his protective arms were around me.

After receiving his kiss on my forehead and hearing him tell me he loved me, I thought that finally, I had my brother back. It was a wonderful feeling and one that I clung to throughout the torment of the days that followed. It was the one thought that kept me going. *My brother loves me. He kissed me on the forehead...he kissed me on the forehead.*

My body was a mess. I had barely survived an operation to put together my broken pelvis, which was now held together with over twenty nuts and bolts; my left arm was fractured, and my left wrist was broken. All of my ribs were fractured, my lungs were punctured and had to be drained of fluid, my collarbone was broken, and I had only just managed to fight off a sepsis infection, which the doctors had been certain would kill me. There were tubes in my throat and up my nostrils feeding me oxygen, liquids, and nourishment. Needles and cannulas were stuck in my right hand, and all around me, machines were bleeping and recording my vital signs in an effort to keep me alive.

I was only vaguely aware of the visitors who travelled from far and wide to be at my bedside. My best friend, Pramod, flew twenty-four hours from the Cayman Islands to be with me, and my good friends Maheshbhai and Vinaben, who happened to be on holiday in Rajkot, came to visit me often. Vinaben later told me that whenever I regained consciousness, my concern was only for my parents. "I am lucky to be alive," I would mumble. "But my parents, they did not make it."

My brother came to see me on one other occasion to tell me that Mum and Dad's funeral had taken place. My heart was shattered into a million pieces, not only because I knew I would never see them again but because I had been unable to say my final goodbyes at their funeral. But still, I hoped my brother had come back to me. The memory of his kiss on my forehead was the only glimmer of warmth in the cold stone of my grief.

By the twenty-fifth day, the doctors in the private hospital had given up on me. "There's nothing more we can do for him," they said. "He needs to be taken to a bigger hospital in Bombay, Delhi, or London."

My fate was in God's hands. But it was also in the hands of someone else.

TWENTY-SEVEN

"He who delivers another from danger, and he who removes terror from the mind, are the greatest of friends."

-   *Hindu saying*

Although I had decided on my return journey from Mumbai that Suji and I were perhaps not meant to be romantically involved, I had not been able to tell her of my decision, as I had sworn to myself I would talk to her face to face when I got back to London and not via text or Whatsapp. The accident put paid to any sort of conversation, and while I was fighting for my life in hospital, Suji was becoming increasingly upset at my lack of replies to her messages. But as soon as news of the accident reached her, she didn't hesitate. She flew straight out to India to be by my side and take charge of the whole situation. In fact, she did so much more than that. She showed true friendship and uncon- ditional love for me that never wavered. She fought for me, supported me, comforted me, believed in me, and gave me back my life. And although we were never destined to be together in a romantic sense, she was the truest friend I could ever have wished for, and I will forever be in her debt.

On my twenty-fifth day in the hospital, when the doctors told Suji they had done all they could for me, she didn't take the news calmly. "You don't know what you're talking about," she fumed before storming out of the meeting to stand by my bedside with her hands on her hips and a look of determination on her face. "Right," she said. "Get your arse out of that bed!"

Of course, I couldn't move, and I was still barely conscious.

Suji broke down in tears. "I don't know what to do," she sobbed. "But I'm not going to let them give up on you. I'm going to get you home, Mayur, and you're going to get better!"

An air ambulance was organised to fly me back to London, and unbeknownst to me, my cousin Mitesh called my brother to have a stern word. "Who is paying for the air ambulance to bring Mayur home?" he asked. "Are me and my siblings going to pay for it, or are you?"

Not wanting to risk being humiliated, my brother reluctantly agreed to pay the costs of £79,000. I was totally unaware of all this and was only vaguely conscious of being wheeled out of the hospital on a stretcher towards the ambulance waiting to take me to the airport, surrounded by crowds of family, medical staff, and well-wishers all there to see me off. Many were in tears, especially my cousins, who had no idea if I would survive the journey or if they would ever see me again. My cousin Vishal's two best friends, Baijoo and Parth, had become very close to me and I to them. They were there too, to see me off. I remember Baijoo running off to fetch some bananas for Suji to take on the plane as she was practicing fasting, eating only fruit, as a symbolic act of sacrifice to God, a mark of her devotion and a way of praying for my recovery. It is strange that out of everything that happened that day, my most vivid memory is of bananas.

I was later told that my send-off was reminiscent of one of the most recognisable moments of a Hindu marriage ceremony, the Vidaai. This emotional ritual occurs when the bride's family bids farewell to their daughter as she rides away with her new husband. In the old days, this ritual was particularly poignant, as the bride would be taken off to her new husband's village and would quite literally never see her family again.

TWENTY-EIGHT

"The road to recovery may be tough, but I've closed all the door that lead to giving up. With only one choice in hand, I am focussed on healing."

- *Vijaya Gowrisankar*

I remember little about the flight back to London. I guess I was heavily sedated for the journey because when I regained consciousness, I was in a bed in Barnet Hospital, with no memory of how I got there. The days passed slowly and painfully, with Suji almost constantly by my side. Because I had only known her for a relatively short time before the accident, my family and friends were not well acquainted with Suji. But this did not stop her from becoming the main point of contact for me. Everybody communicated through her, and everybody could see what a truly wonderful person she was and how well she was taking care of me.

Because of the tube inserted in my throat, I couldn't even

speak during those first few weeks in hospital. When friends visited, I had to communicate by spelling out words on the backs of their hands, which was exhausting. My best friend Pramod and his wife Sulaksha, who both loved me like a brother, were regular visitors and a godsend to me. They encouraged me, lifted my spirits, and generally showered me in their love, care, and attention. Suji and Sulaksha were like two peas in a pod in the way they looked after me.

I would have these slow conversations with Pramod, him asking questions and me spelling out the answers on his hand or a board printed with the letters of the alphabet. One day, I spelled out I had something very, very important to tell him. My finger laboriously spelled out the first couple of words before I was overcome with exhaustion and fell asleep, leaving poor Pramod to shout in frustration, "What is so important, Mayur? What is so important?"

One day, when I was finally able to croak out a few words, I asked Suji if she would call my brother for me. The whole time I had been in hospital in the UK, he had only visited me once, and that had only been because my son had wanted to see me. That my brother had not visited since weighed heavily on me. "Are you sure you want me to call?" asked Suji.

I nodded.

When my brother answered the call, it was painful and difficult to get the words out. "Bhai," I finally managed to say. "Listen to me. I have a brother who once bought me a leather jacket with his very first pay packet. A brother who, when he found out the weather had turned cold in Wales, sent me two jumpers, one green and one blue, with a message saying, *keep warm, brother.* I have a brother who flew 5,000 miles to kiss me on the forehead and say, *I love you. I'll be here for you. Nothing's going to happen to you. I promise to look after you.*

Will this brother not come to visit me now when I am only twenty minutes away?"

"I will think about it," came his reply.

I knew this meant no. I had heard the phrase many times before from my ex-wife. The phone call, and the way my brother spoke to me, plunged me into a dark place. Could the man on the phone be the same brother who had told me he loved me? It felt as though I had lost him all over again.

Finally, the day came when I was lucid enough to chat about my condition with the doctor. All I wanted to know was how soon it would be before I could walk out of the hospital and go home. The doctor took his time before answering carefully. "Don't be in such a hurry," he said at first. "You need to take things one day at a time." Then he cleared his throat and spoke to me gently. "I am sorry to say, but in my honest opinion, you may not ever walk again."

His words were a dagger in my heart. For a moment, I was struck dumb as my mind raced to comprehend what the doctor had just told me and what it would mean for my future. Then suddenly, I remembered the words the motivational speaker Joseph McClendon III had spoken on hearing his mother had been diagnosed with terminal cancer. "I'm very sorry to tell you," the

doctor had told him. "But your mother has about two to three months of life left before the cancer takes her."

McClendon had swallowed hard, stunned and speechless as anyone would be. Then he looked the doctor in the eye and said back to him. "Doctor, I appreciate your diagnosis, but I will not accept your verdict." McClendon had been studying the effects of good nutrition on the human body for some years and was determined not to accept his mother's fate quietly. He decided there and then to dedicate his life to finding a way to help his mother beat the disease that threatened her life. His mother lived for a further eleven and a half years, thanks to her son not giving up on her.

With the words of my own doctor ringing in my ears - *you may never walk again, Mayur* - I took a leaf from McClendon's book and repeated his phrase. "Doctor, I appreciate your diagnosis, but I will not accept your verdict."

That evening, I told Suji what the doctor had said and how I had replied. "I will walk again," I told her. "And not only that, I will run another marathon."

She looked at me as though I had gone completely mad. "You must be hallucinating again," she said jokingly.

But I wasn't hallucinating. I was deadly serious. There and then, I made a solemn vow, that come what may, in three years, I was going to run another marathon. And when I saw the doctor again the next day, I thanked him for motivating me. He nodded, smiled at me, and said, "That's the spirit, Mayur. That's the spirit."

The hours passed slowly, lying in my hospital bed. I replayed conversations over and over again in my head - particularly those I had with Mum when I had opened my heart to her in India. I closed my eyes and relived every word.

I had plenty of time to contemplate, and when the realisation dawned that Papa was no longer a punchbag; he was no longer suffering in humiliation and indignity, my anger evaporated like the final wisps of a spent storm cloud disappearing into thin air. A feeling of forgiveness for my brother descended upon me. Let his karma deal with him as per the rules, I thought. I even started sending him birthday wishes again on the family WhatsApp group. The bitterness had gone. Whilst listening to lectures of Swami Parthasarathy, another realisation dawned on me. Before, there had been a part of me that wanted my brother punished for ruining my life and for beating Papa, but this feeling was no longer inside me. The love in my heart for my brother was still there as it had always been. Just as it will always be there for Yudhister towards Duryodhan, even if he had very little respect for Duryodhan and Sakuni.

As for my four candles, the words of Nelson Mandela kept on springing to mind. "I have walked a long walk to freedom. It has been a lonely road. And it is not over yet. I know that (my four candles) were not meant to carry hatred. No one is born hating another person. People learn to hate. They can be taught to love. For love comes more naturally to the human heart."

If my four candles have the courage to understand, they will know that I did nothing wrong except hold on to the truth and righteousness. And this they can only comprehend once the truth explodes.

As I lay in my hospital bed wracked with pain, it came to me that only now, after becoming physically disabled, had I learned to be mentally able. But this new inner strength had arrived at a great price. I swore that although I might only be a minority of one, I would live happily with the attitude of holding on to the truth and fighting for justice and righteousness.

With all the endless hours, days, and weeks of sleeping, dreaming, hallucinating, and battling with pain and grief, my mind had nothing better to do than to think constantly of my four candles and the web of silence, lies, and misinter-pretation that led to our estrangement. Over and over again, like a video on replay, my thoughts tormented me.

For years I stayed quiet about my daughter's DNA to

protect her from the world. Even in the courtroom, I remained silent. But then, at the second hearing, I realised my silence was not protecting her. It was only increasing the avalanche of lies. It was increasing the negative karma on my four candles.

Contemplating all this in my hospital bed, I knew that raising my voice would destroy the peace in their minds and my mind. But not raising it would destroy the self-integrity and dignity of my four candles by condemning them to live lives of lies. If the few people who knew the truth did not fight for the truth, then who would protect my four candles from the lies bestowed upon their naive and innocent hearts and minds?

Everything comes with a price. Fighting for the truth comes at a massive cost.

Lying there in the hospital, I vowed that, come what may, I would hold my head up with dignity in doing what needed to be done, even in the knowledge that the price paid would be costly and painful. If I took the coward's way out, I would die in a safer environment as a coward, but lies and unrighteous lives would prevail in the Kotecha family. I realised this still might be the case if my four candles were also cowards by not having the courage to face the proven truths. More than anything, I wanted my four candles and their future spouses and the generations to come to live lives free from lies. If those kings on the battlefield of

Kurukshetra and their armies could lay down their lives for an injustice done to just six people, why couldn't I do this for my own four candles?

I knew for certain that in time to come, I would cross the finishing line of the London Marathon, collect my medal and bring it back to the hospital to show the doctor proudly. But more importantly, I thought again about the other marathon, the marathon of life that stretched out in front of me. I remembered the words of Martin Luther King, "Injustice anywhere is a threat to justice everywhere." I knew I had two choices. I either did not enter the marathon of life for the truth to reach my four candles or if I committed to entering, then I could not stop for anything. No matter the intensity of pain I might endure, or even if my legs broke, the race had to be completed once started. As in the Mahabharat, when Krishna recited the Bhagavad-Gita to Arjun on the battlefield of Kurukshetra – winning or losing was secondary.

I knew the marathon of life had become a priority for me. I knew I needed to keep battling for the truth and the righteousness of my four candles. Even if they chose to defeat their own righteousness because they had no courage to contemplate the facts, I would keep running until my very last breath. If I fell, I would get up and run again. And if I fell again, I would get up again and again. Not only for me and my four candles but also for all those fathers and children who have been denied justice. For all the battered parents who have physically and silently suffered by the hands of the ones they gave life to. Washing my dirty laundry in public was not the issue; allowing truth and righteousness to surface was. And if anyone had a problem with that, could they really be truthful and righteous? And if they were righteous, they should not be afraid of the truth. If they still had a problem, it was their problem and not mine.

For too long, lies, dishonesty, and unrighteousness had been winning. But, no more. My conscience could relax now. I could take a deep breath and expose my truth. What everyone else involved did with the truth was up to them. They could deny it further, cover it with more lies, and have no courage to face the facts. It was up to them. Hopefully, they would not want to expose their character if they further denied the truth and then it exploded into the open.

Even if I did not win my children back and my heart lost, at least my intellect and conscience would win knowing I did the right thing. In my life coaching classes, I always said to people, "Let it be said you won. Let it be said that you lost. Do not let it be said that you lost by default by not playing when you really wanted to." I would play for the truth to win.

Whether the intentions of those who led my four candles to live lives of lies was right or wrong, the decision to act on righteousness had to come from them. And it could only come when they faced the truth. I had the right to love all

262

four of my candles from a distance, and they had the right to choose their direction in life - towards righteousness or lies. That was their choice. But the more the truth was opposed, the taller I would stand and the louder I would shout for the truth.

And the truth would eventually come out. It is thinner than water, after all. I understood the devastation that my four angels would feel when that happened, how their faith and trust in those who taught them to be upholders of faith and trust would be shattered. And how their anger towards me would initially increase for exposing what they believe are lies. And there was the risk that, most likely, rather than accept the truth, they would choose a life of lies and, by doing so, would condemn their souls and those of their spouses and children.

For my son to live without his father was painful enough, but for him to live without dignity would be even more devastating

Had my four candles still hated me after hearing and seeing proof of the truth from both sides, it would have been understandable. But they hated me after hearing only lies from one side, which I could prove were lies. That was an injustice done towards me, and I had to correct it with an act of justice. And if my four candles did not have the courage to be righteous even after that, then, I thought, let it all be buried.

My mistake had been in thinking I would wait until my children were old enough to understand before explaining everything to them. I did not realise how they would be manipulated, brainwashed, and unable to contemplate the proven truth. I should have exposed the injustice from the very beginning. Many fathers who have suffered this kind of injustice are also guilty of allowing themselves to be humiliated to protect their offspring and thus condemn their children to live in a world of deep lies. If I did not take a stance, I would be sending a message to the future wives of three of my candles that it was acceptable to be manipulative and indulge in extra-marital affairs. That it is okay to be punched by your children in your old age. The message I wanted to send was to tell them to be braver than me in upholding the truth and self-respect.

For all that I did wrong, I had and would ask for forgiveness. I would, with palms together, even beg for forgiveness. But for the things I knew I was right about, I would stand up for righteousness and justice and for the truth to come out. And, if they had an ounce of righteousness in them, they would have the courage to uphold their own dignity by accepting the proven truth without fear, without bowing to anyone, without hiding away. It took me a very long time to realise this. I did not want my three princes to make the same mistakes as me. I did not want them to keep quiet and bear the lies and injustice. It took me years to realise that the fire should have been extinguished when it first sparked up.

But once it got out of hand, myself and my four candles got burnt in a life of lies and karmic destruction. If they had self-dignity, they would not be afraid of facing the truth. They should have faith in themselves and move forward in the light of the truth.

It was a mystery to me why the people who committed the unrighteous deeds wanted to hide the truth so as not to be ashamed of it, even though it was a truth they created. If three out of the four parents of my four candles had chosen to immerse their children in the world of unrighteousness and lies, then the chance of the fourth parent - me – bringing the truth into the light would be slim, especially as I was hated for reasons that were lies. Should that stop me from attempting to get the truth out? Should the other three parents be punished? Not by me nor their children, but by the truth coming out, their children being given proof of the truth and then upholding it.

I only went to see my son at university because I did not want to regret not giving him the chance to live the truth. I didn't want my four candles to think of themselves too weak to live by the truth. They were not weak. They could, if they wished to, choose to be righteous.

These thoughts crowded my head, minute by minute and hour by hour, as I fought to heal my body. I knew the time had come for me to find an opportune time and way to get the truth to my four candles. If I failed and they continued to be cowards, I would carry on looking for opportune moments until the day they finally found the courage. Their three other parents should not be punished, as all of us had done many things wrong. They could even be respected and admired, like John Newton, if they chose to abandon lies and wrongfulness for truth and righteousness. My ex-wife, my brother, and his wife wanted to put 'The End' between my four candles and myself in order to bury the truth. But the truth is thinner than water. It would come out eventually. Still, the eternal question remained. Had they weakened so much that they no longer had the courage and strength to stand up for the truth and be heroes within themselves? Concealing the truth is as big a sin as lying, I thought. But no matter how bitter the truth is or how hard, the truth is the truth and nothing else. And nothing else is the truth but the truth.

I felt so strongly that Mum had only been waiting for some closure between us before moving on. Luckily and miraculously, we had achieved that only half an hour before the accident. Although she never got the chance to fulfil her promise of speaking to my son, I knew her spiritual strength was somehow helping me to reach my four candles.

TWENTY-NINE

"There are hundreds of paths up the mountain, all leading to the same place, so it doesn't matter what path you take. The only person wasting time is the one who runs around the mountain, telling everyone that his or her path is wrong."

-   *Hindu Proverb*

I spent two months in Barnet Hospital being pumped full of five different antibiotics daily to battle a superbug that had insinuated itself within the metal pins that had been bolted into my pelvis while in hospital in India. Soon after, I was transferred to the Royal London Hospital in preparation for a touch and go operation to remove the infection. But I was very weak and needed regular infusions of potassium and other nutrients to build up my strength. My feeding tubes had been removed, and I could eat by mouth again, the only problem being that I rejected every meal offered to me. I had no appetite. I just couldn't face anything, and I had lost 40% of my body weight. The doctors even threatened to insert the feeding tube back in my nostrils if I didn't eat something soon.

My auntie, Mum's eldest sister, Taramasi, kept bringing all sorts of home-cooked morsels to tempt me, as well as fruits and all manner of treats. But nothing seemed to whet my appetite. Then one day, she brought in a bottle of Ribena, and for some reason, I suddenly thought I would quite like to drink a glass of it. I managed a few sips, and as the sweet, blackcurrant flavour of childhood flooded my mouth, my taste buds woke up, and my interest in drinking gradually returned.

One night I dreamt I was at my cricket club. It was a hot day. The sun was streaming down, the smell of freshly cut grass was in the air, and in my hand was an ice-cold glass bottle of Coke. I could feel the ice droplets nestling in the contours of the iconic glass bottle, and my mouth watered. I tipped the bottle to my mouth and heard the crisp fizz of the bubbles before the sweet sharpness of the drink hit my tongue. Then I gulped down a few mouthfuls, and it was the most delicious and refreshing thing I had ever tasted.

When I woke, the dream was still so vivid, and I mentioned it to a nurse who was kind enough to bring me her own Coke to try. It tasted just as good as in my dream, and later that day, Suji brought me in my very own bottles, making sure they were the original glass bottles just as I had dreamt.

Slowly, slowly, with my taste buds now awakened, my

appetite grew. I could eat small amounts at breakfast at first. Then a little bit of lunch, and gradually, some of my strength returned. The doctors thought I was finally strong enough to have the operation to remove the infected metal in my pelvis. But because The Royal London is home to London's Air Ambulance and the capital's leading trauma and emergency care centre, my operation was cancelled six times due to more urgent cases being flown in. From my bed, I could see the familiar red helicopters coming in to land on a regular basis, and my heart went out to the victims inside, knowing that for them to be in the air ambulance at all meant their injuries were significant.

By some good fortune, by the time the next slot for an operation became available, the doctors found that the antibiotics, my immune system, and my mental strength had beaten the infection into submission, and there was no need for an operation after all.

Along with all the other injuries I had to contend with, while in hospital in India, I had developed a bedsore on my back, as at that time, the doctors were unable to move me because of the tubes in my body keeping me alive. By the time I arrived at The Royal London Hospital, the bedsore had grown to the size of a mobile phone, and the nurse could fit her fist inside. I was hooked up to a wound VAC to assist the healing process. A gauze dressing was placed directly on my wound with an adhesive film to seal the dressing and wound. A drainage pump led from under the adhesive film, which was in turn connected to a portable vacuum pump. The gases in the air around us put pressure on the surface of our bodies. A wound vacuum device removes this pressure over the area of a wound. This can help a wound heal in several ways. It can gently pull fluid from the wound over time, reducing swelling, and may help clean the wound and remove bacteria. A wound VAC also helps pull the edges of the wound together. And it may stimulate the growth of new tissue that helps the wound to heal. But it was obviously excruciating. It was painful to sleep on my back or my side, and in any case, I had to be moved from my left side to my right every two hours.

To distract me from the pain, Suji or Sulaksha would bring in cards and letters from family and well-wishers that had been sent to my home and read them out loud to me. Sulaksha was doing this one day, and just listening to all the kind words that people had sent was making me feel better. As she worked her way through the pile of post, she came to one letter, and after skimming the contents, I noticed a frown cross her face. "We won't worry about that one," she said and put it to the bottom of the pile.

"What is it?" I asked.

"No, really," she said. "Forget that one."

But I wouldn't take no for an answer. "Please," I said. "Tell me what it is."

She sighed and very reluctantly told me it was a letter from my brother's solicitor demanding that I pay him back the sum of £99,000 – the cost of flying me back from India. At that moment, the pain in my heart eclipsed the agony of all my injuries.

"I'll pay him," I said. "If that's what's important to him when his only brother is lying in hospital in excruciating pain, then I'll pay him."

But Pramod would not hear of it. As a barrister, he took charge of the letter and reassured me he would deal with the whole matter. So many of my relatives and friends were disgusted when they heard what my brother had done. I found out later from my cousin Mitesh that my brother was actually only £47,000 out of pocket. Yet there he was, demanding £99,000 from me. My heart was broken. I was also to learn that while I lay helplessly disabled in hospital, my Dad's name was removed from Mum and Dad's post office in South London and from their land in Kent to deprive me of my inheritance. An attempt was also made to remove Dad's name from the main house. Thankfully this attempt was discovered in time, but only because a letter arrived at the house addressed to Mum from the land registry office saying that a request had been made to have her and Dad's name removed from the house.

Soon after, because I no longer needed an operation, I was transferred to a local hospital, Northwick Park Hospital, which was closer to home.

After seven months in various hospitals, I was eventually moved to Woodland Hall Rehabilitation Centre in Stanmore. My progress was slow, but sure. One of my therapies involved being strapped to a tilt table that was gradually raised to reintroduce my body to a vertical position and encourage weight-bearing. One day, one of my best friend's children (my angels, as I called them), Priyanka, witnessed me being raised 80%, almost upright for the first time in many months. Because of my height and my ability to pluck an apple from a tree, another of my angels, Avni, had given me the nickname Giraffe Uncle, and my other angels soon followed suit. I was so proud that day for Priyanka to see her Giraffe Uncle almost at full height again.

Then came the momentous day when I walked two yards from my bed to a chair with the assistance of a gutter frame. The pain was intense as I had developed drop feet due to the accident and from months of being bed-bound. This condition made it difficult for me to lift the front part of my feet, so they dragged along the floor. It was yet another thing for me to overcome, but it didn't take away from the immense feeling of pride that flooded through me. I only wished that Mum and Dad could have been there to witness this small but incredible victory of mine.

Every day, still with the assistance of a gutter frame, I took a few more steps until from two yards I was walking thirty yards. From the gutter frame, I was moved onto a zimmer frame, although I was reluctant to do so at first, as a zimmer frame didn't give me as much support. Then finally, the day came when I was deemed fit enough to return home. It didn't seem possible, yet at the same time, everything now seemed possible.

THIRTY

"He does not live in vain; who employs his wealth, his thought, and his speech to advance the good of others."

- *Hindu Proverb*

Almost a year after boarding my flight to India, and with eight months of that time spent in hospital, I finally stood outside my home again. I was overwhelmed with emotions. When the door was opened for me, and I was helped inside, I knew that there would be no Mummy to greet and no Papa to hug. All their belongings would be inside just as they had left them before travelling to India to meet me. I didn't know if I could bear it.

But again, my good friends and family rallied around. Suji, her best friend Neena, her husband Dominic, and their two children Aaron and Aneka, my cousin's sister Binta, and niece Grishma were all there to welcome me home. They had organised a homecoming pizza party in my honour, and I was more grateful than they could ever have imagined for their love, care, thoughtfulness, and company on such a challenging occasion.

The hospital driver helped me climb the two steps into the house as my friends videoed the occasion. Once inside, I walked over to Dad's chair and sat down in it, knowing it would always be my chair now. I managed to keep my tears at bay to eat some pizza with everybody, and after they left, Suji went upstairs to sleep in my old room, while I went to sleep in a hospital bed that had been set up for me in what had been Mum's living room. It was then that I let my tears flow freely. All that had happened in the past long, horrific months came crashing down on me like a mountain of rocks. Now that I was back in our home, the absence of Mum and Dad became real, and grief overwhelmed me. I cried and cried that first night and many nights afterwards, but in the midst of my sorrow, I vowed I would make my parents so proud of me. Firstly, I would keep fighting for the truth for the sake of my four candles and their future generations. Secondly, I would keep fighting to regain my health and use of my body and, come what may, would confound all the doctors and their expectations and complete the next London Marathon.

For the first four weeks at home, carers visited me every day, and my intense physiotherapy sessions continued. Suji had arranged for an occupational therapist to assess the house and my needs and install all necessary disability equipment. Every day I grew a little stronger. And every day, I looked at the beautiful smiling faces of Mum and Dad in the photograph that Suji had printed out and hung in pride of place on the wall. The two people I had spent thirty wonderful days in India with were no longer with me, but I could still feel their presence in the house and their blessings showering down on me. And I was comforted to know that Mummy and Papa had been closer to each other during those precious thirty days in their beloved country than they had been in the past thirty years.

Every day presented me with a new challenge. And every day, I faced the challenge with positivity, determination, and usually, a great splash of humour. By the beginning of June 2020, I ventured outside to walk on my own two feet. It was a defining moment, even though I still needed the support of crutches or walking sticks to keep me upright once I stopped. Before long, I could kick a football while balanced on my crutches, and then a great day indeed arrived, and a breakthrough for my independence, when I managed to drive my car again. And my first journey was to the gym!

In February 2021, I received the amazing news that I would be running the London Marathon for the London Air Ambulance Service. Now things got serious, and my determination and training really stepped up. I walked through rain and mud, up and down hills, and through woods and fields, building my stamina and pace with every tentative step. When I returned home exhausted, I would find some peace in the beautiful shrine my cousin Manish had helped me create in the garden for my parents, my living gods.

My friends and the majority of my family continued to be awesome, visiting me regularly and encouraging me along the way. Although my relationship with Suji went no further than great friends, I could never come anywhere close to repaying her for all she did for me. She literally saved my life, and I could never thank her enough for her love, generosity, kindness, and devotion. She is truly one of a kind, and I am blessed to have her as a dear and hugely valued friend.

After my relationship with Suji ended, I decided to have some counselling. I realised that I had formed a habit of ending relationships. Why was my trust so easily broken? And what could I do about it? As soon as I opened up to the counsellor about my past, she immediately recognised the problem. Because of everything that had happened between Sia and me, I had developed huge trust issues. In addition, she made me realise for the first time that how my brother had acted towards me was a form of abuse. His bullying of me from a young age had made me feel useless and had destroyed my confidence and self-worth. I often thought of the Albert Einstein quote, "Everybody is a genius, but if you judge a fish by its ability to climb a tree, it will live its whole life believing it is stupid." All my life, my brother had made me feel like a stupid fish. But I was never destined to climb a tree. I was destined to swim.

With the help of my counsellor, I was finally able to accept that risk comes with learning to trust again. None of us are perfect. All of us let other people down sometimes. I had to learn to take emotional risks, to learn how trust works and that it isn't given out freely. I had to face my fears and other negative feelings built around trust. Quite simply, I had to try and trust again.

I swore I was never going to allow myself to be abused again. I was not going to live by the opinions of others or allow them to bully me. In short, I was not going to let my past affect my future ever again.

THIRTY-ONE

"Parents are the God in the world of your life. Under their protection lies your destiny of future. Upon their sweet will, our delight is evergreen that the world has to cherish and consider. One must be very obedient to our parents and pray for their good life and always have the will to prostrate deep into them. We did not feel their presence when they are moving before our eyes, but the moment they are away from our life, we immediately realise their importance."

-   *Salvation by Lord Shri Krishna*

The day of the London Marathon draws ever closer, and my days are organised to fit in as much training as possible. My personal trainer Lili, who trained me for the marathon in 2016, loves to see me in pain! She challenges me to the very edge and beyond of my physical capabilities. She is a fantastic trainer and a much-loved friend who has enormous faith in me and has managed to make me believe my body is capable of the most amazing things.

On Mondays and Fridays, I train in the gym for ever-increasing amounts of time, and on Wednesdays, I run ever-increasing distances with the help of two Nordic sticks. On Thursdays and Saturdays, I work as a volunteer delivering food to the vulnerable and elderly, and on Tuesdays, I do my paperwork and the shopping for Dad's sister, Indufai. Also, on a Friday, I manage to fit in meeting the lads again at the local cricket club. Then Sunday is a day to relax, contemplate and plan for the future. But every morning, as soon as I wake up, the first thing I do is burn an incense stick in front of the photograph of Mum and Dad and ask for their blessing and forgiveness.. I let them know that I am happy, and like a little boy, I tell them of all my achievements. "Be happy where you are," I say to them. "And know that I am happy." Then I turn to Lord Yogeshwar (another name for Krishna) and ask him to please look after my first Gods and make sure they are happy. Only when all this is done can my day begin.

Only recently, and only since I have been able to walk upstairs again, have I been able to bring myself to sort through my parents' belongings and decide what to do with everything. It bought a smile to my face that when I collected together all Dad's clothes, his coat, trousers, and jumpers, etc. (none of which were brand new or designer label, unless you count M&S as designer!) including some of my own clothes, I filled three black bin bags. Yet with Mum's vast and immaculate collection of saris, I filled seventeen black bin bags! I have decided to let Mum's sisters have the first choice of the saris, and the rest I will send over to India for the needy. I think Mum, and certainly, Dad would approve.

That my living Gods departed this earth on Mahashivratri, the most auspicious day of Lord Shivji, brings great comfort to me. I like to believe Lord Shivji himself came to collect them, and neither of them had to stand in judgement before Yamraj, the God of Death, who, although feared by the living, plays a vital role in maintaining the balance of the world through the continuous cycle of life and death. When a person's life span runs out, the soul of the dead is brought before him, and Yamraj passes judgment according to the deeds carried out on the earthly plane, upon which he then decides the fate of the dead. The souls of sinners are sent to one of many hells. The virtuous are reunited with their forefathers. Often, a person's soul is returned to earth to accomplish more good deeds so they can eventually be reunited with their forefathers.

I hoped that by passing from this life on Mahashivratri, my parents had already achieved karmic balance, and as the last line in the famous bhajan says, "not you Yamraj, but you, my Lord Shivji will come to collect me." Shivji might be known as the 'destroyer,' but that is because he destroys all impurities that reside in the human, rids a body of its shortcomings, liberating it from the cycle of birth and death, making it worthy to attain salvation or moksha.

My first and foremost wish is that my parents have broken the cycle of life and death, and they are living in eternal happiness in a state of Self-realisation. If that is not possible, my second wish is that I do not attain Self-realisation before them and that they are my parents in every life so that I can make amends for all the mistakes I've made towards them. I pray, too, that one day there will be closure between my four candles and me, and my brother and me.

I am excited about the future. I am excited to complete the marathon. And when Covid restrictions are finally relaxed, I am excited to get my teeth into a new project that I know would fill Mum and Dad's hearts with such pride and joy. With the wealth left to me by Dad in India, I plan to launch Authentic India. It is a business project based on Vedic principles designed to empower the women of rural villages in India by creating small cottage industry hubs for traditional Indian crafts such as handmade soaps, blankets, incense sticks, copperware, and pottery to be sold on Amazon. This will, in turn, finance Girl Empowerment, where the education of girls will be funded from a young age up to master degree level. Any money I make will be ploughed back into the project to benefit the girls and women of the Gujarat villages. This project will give my life a purpose and a focus away from daily nerve pain and other trivial challenges. I have been planning and preparing for this since I was in hospital, and have since completed an online course on selling via Amazon. I have learned how to conduct business by employing the philosophy of Vedic culture, prepared my team, and formulated a ten-year plan in accordance with 'Governing Business and Relationships' by Swami Parthasarathy. After not only cheating death, but then going on to complete the London Marathon, I am full of confidence in my abilities to succeed in this endeavour. I pray my greatest strength will come from the blessings of my parents. This project will also allow me to pay homage to Mummy and Papa – my first Gods.

And of course, I have also spent the last few months writing this book. The process of putting words onto pages allowed me to have a final conversation with my beautiful parents, to pour my heart out, and commemorate the last 30 Days in Heaven I was privileged enough to spend with them. It was a very painful process at times, but it was also wonderful to revisit such happy memories and speak the truth at last. On occasion, I was filled with doubt over the wisdom of laying bare my heart and soul, but I couldn't live with being silenced anymore. This book is a love letter to my wonderful Mummy and Papa, pure and simple. Over and over again, the sentence 'salvation lies in service at the feet of your parents' runs through my head. And I know that never a truer sentence has been written.

I hope all of you who read this book will smile and remember your first Gods with love and respect and find the courage to open your hearts too.

"If you want to see brave, look at those who can forgive."

-Bhagwad Gita

EPILOGUE

On Sunday, October 3, 2021, I completed the 41st London Marathon in 11 hours, 14 minutes, and 30 seconds, raising to date over £3,000 in aid of London's Air Ambulance. I sustained a groin injury just before the 2-mile mark, so I walked the remaining 24 miles instead of keeping up a gentle jog despite being in great pain. For the first 9 miles, I walked with the aid of a pair of Nordic walking sticks. I then found an abandoned supermarket shopping trolley which I used as support until the final 3 miles when I returned to using the Nordic sticks.

I am so proud to say that not only did I fulfil my vow to complete the London Marathon - despite being told by doctors that I would never walk again - but I also had the honour of being the very last person to cross the finishing line.

ACKNOWLEDGEMENTS

I would like to thank my wonderful friend Suji Gohil, the main hero of my story. I would not be here today without your tremendous love, support, tenacity, loyalty, and encouragement through my most challenging moments. There are no words big enough or long enough to express my gratitude for all you have done for me. I will be forever in your debt.

A million thank yous to my wonderful friends and family, Pramod Joshi and Sulakshana Joshi (my best friend and his wife, my soul sister), my cousin Vishal Ashvinbhai Selani, also Hitesh Purohit, Anjana Lad, and my aunt Indu Badiani. And not forgetting my nephew, Rishi Thobani, and Giraffe Uncle's angels, Priyanka, Shivani, Keshav, Avni, and Eva. I am so hugely grateful to you all for your love, support, patience, and generosity. Equally to Suji's son Kian for supporting both his mum and me while she was supporting me.

Huge thanks also to Usha Kant, Maheshbhai Kukadia, Vina Kukadia, Liliana Focşa, Manish Jobanputra, Binta Bhuptani. Mitesh Badiani, Nimisha Mehan, and Sheetal

Badiani. Also to the South London boys Rajesh, Alpesh, Alkesh, Amar, Vinil, Jeeva, Shilpav, Vimal, Nrupesh, and Mahendrabhai.

Special thanks to Pandurang Shastri Athavale, founder of Swadhyay Parivar and all associated with Swadhyay Parivar particularly, Shirishbhai Joshi, Keshavjibhai Bhanderi, Ramaben Bhanderi, and Atul Pancholi.

I am, of course, indebted to and hugely thankful for all the fantastic nurses, doctors, and staff who looked after me in various hospitals in India, the UK, and the rehabilitation centre.

Thank you also to Vijay Kanani and Rupal Mehta for giving me honest feedback on this book. Your wisdom and insight were truly valuable.

A huge thank you to my writing partner Alison Rattle for her inspiration and creativity with words. And to Steve Eggleston, India Roberts and Michael Powell for making this book possible.

Massive thanks to my Four Candles, Avni, Nikhil, Arjun and Ravni.

Finally, and above all, thank you to my beloved parents and my grandmother.

ABOUT THE AUTHORS

MAYUR KOTECHA was born in Mwanza, Tanzania, but has lived in the UK since he was eight. He is a successful property developer as well as a qualified business and life coach, and his passions include history and travelling across India. A life changing accident in 2019 inspired him to write 30 Days in Heaven and continues to inspire him in his latest project, Authentic India, which focuses on Village, Women, and Girl Empowerment.

ALISON RATTLE has co-authored eleven non-fiction titles for Barnes & Noble, Michael O'Mara, Prion Books, and Andre Deutsch, and has published four fiction titles for Hot Key Books. She has a MA (distinction) in Writing for Young People, was long-listed for the Brandford Boase Award, and nominated for the NETB Award and Leeds Book Award. She has written for The Guardian and appeared on radio and TV, including ITV's Martina Cole's Lady Killers series. She works in a diverse capacity for Eggman Global Agency and Hummingbird Publishing. She lives with her husband on a narrowboat in Wiltshire, England.

OTHER BOOKS FROM HUMMINGBIRD PUBLISHING AUTHORS

Alison Rattle
Amelia Dyer: Angel Maker
V for Violet
The Quietness
The Madness
The Beloved

Steve Eggleston
Conquering Your Adversaries
Writing Your Book After Covid-19
Destination 9/11
Conflicted
A Long Way Home

Michael Powell
The Little Book of Dumb Questions
Games on Thrones
Forbidden Knowledge
Mind Games
Smarties Guide to the Galaxy

hummingbird-publishing.com

AVAILABLE TO BUY NOW FROM

HUMMINGBIRD PUBLISHING

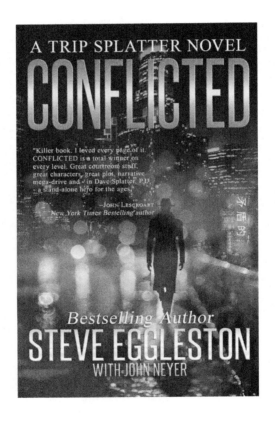

Printed in Great Britain
by Amazon

81283888R00171